THE *MAGIC* OF *CHAMPAGNE*

THE *MAGIC* OF *CHAMPAGNE*

ANDREW JEFFORD

St. Martin's Press
New York

THE MAGIC OF CHAMPAGNE

For information, address St. Martin's Press, 175 Fifth Avenue, New York, NY 10010.

ISBN 0-312-09865-0

Library of Congress Cataloguing-in-Publication data available on request.

First published in the United Kingdom by Webster's Wine Price Guide Ltd,
Axe & Bottle Court, 70 Newcomen Street, London SE1 1YT.

First US Edition: September 1993

Colour separations by Scantrans (PTE) Ltd, Singapore.
Printed and bound by Toppan Printing Co, Singapore.

Conceived, edited and designed by Websters International Publishers.

CONTENTS

CHAMPAGNE

...irrésistible attrait...

INTRODUCTION

Champagne and celebrations go hand-in-hand.
On birthdays or at weddings, for Christmas,
christenings and romantic tête-à-têtes, for
launching boats and books, for setting a seal on
contracts or diplomatic triumphs, for toasting
the winners of motor races, football matches or
elections. When we reach the important
milestones in our lives and whenever we wish to
mark an occasion as something particularly
special, we seek out a unique wine from a quiet,
hilly corner of north-east France – a wine that is
pale gold in colour, clear as ice and sparkles like
stars: champagne. No other, it seems, will do.
The story of this magical wine and the people
who make it is told in the following pages.

*Champagne is, above all, a symbol of elegance and
sophistication – an 'irresistible attraction' according to
this 1949 advertising poster by René Gruau.*

THE IMAGE OF CHAMPAGNE

THE IMAGE OF CHAMPAGNE IS an extraordinarily powerful one. It carries a range of associations so alluring as to be irresistible. No other wine can match them. When we drink champagne we feel elegant and sophisticated, frivolous, chic, light-hearted, carefree, extravagant, reckless, generous, expansive, ready to lay aside for a moment the humdrum demands of everyday life. And it's not just the alcohol that's performing this transformation, for the magic begins to work as soon as the cork

C'était le bon temps !

A drink for kings. A French cartoon shows Edward VII enjoying a glass of his favourite tipple.

pops and the bubbles whoosh into the glass, before even the first sip is taken. Much of this, no doubt, is the result of the cleverest and most sustained advertising campaign in the history of wine, but some of it, at least, is to do with the nature of the wine itself.

The star-drinker

One of the most enduring myths about wine is that Dom Pérignon invented champagne: the first bottle was uncorked, a glass was poured and, standing in the cool darkness of the cellar, the blind monk declared 'I am drinking stars'.

The truth is that no one invented champagne; it just happened. It happened as wine itself happened: as a stage in a natural process, as a frozen moment in the cycle of birth and decay. But it could only happen in a wine-growing area where autumn came quickly, and where winter was chilly, for the natural process in question was the stopping of fermentation by winter cold, and its beginning again when warmer weather came in the spring. The 'second fermentation' put a rush of bubbles into the new wine. This happened regularly in

Champagne sales boomed in the years after World War Two. Film stars like Paulette Goddard were often photographed drinking it, thus adding the wine's glamour to their own.

Champagne; so, when the moment came for winemakers to make the most of this natural process, it was logical that they should do so here. They were simply exploiting a natural resource, just as islanders would set about fishing or those living above coal seams sink mines.

And it worked. This new sort of wine proved extraordinarily successful. It was so successful that a myth was required, a myth about a blind monk who said he was drinking stars. We need stories and myths, when the truth is as unspectacular as evolution.

Why did it work so well? All wine has some dissolved gas in it; if it did not, it would taste flat and dull. But too much gas would tear most wines to pieces. The acid base wines of Champagne, however, become mysteriously ennobled and completed by the charge of gas: their concentration seems to increase; their flavours acquire balance, verve and poise; their penetration and length stretches remarkably.

Naturally, in the minds of drinkers, such a wine assumed a peculiar significance. It was temperamental, unpredictable. It had to be bottled and corked, and the cork firmly muzzled. Lift the muzzle, ease the cork, and it will leap in the air, and the wine will sometimes leap after it. In the glass, it 'quibbles and puns'. In the mouth, it

French racing driver Alain Prost celebrating a victory in traditional effervescent style with a bottle of Moët.

A magnum of Dom Perignon '82 sold at Christie's for £1650 in 1989. Expensive, even for champagne – but because of the engraved bottle, not its contents.

tickles the tongue, freshens the palate and fills the nasal passages with aroma. One sip is soon followed by a second, and a third; the bubbles apparently hurry alcohol into the bloodstream, and a delicious lightheadedness and inexplicable gaiety are soon experienced. Champagne seems, more than any other wine, to have a life of its own: it is impatient and fretful, wilful and high-spirited, charming, more than a little dangerous. Its high price – for this, of all wines, requires lavish time and labour from its maker – intensifies the impression that champagne is special, a wine apart. The high price also ensures that champagne is associated with high living, with the mouthwatering excesses of the rich, the fashionable and the famous.

Image into edifice

If there is one sphere of business in which the French, as a nation, are supremely skilled, it is in the making and marketing of luxury products. Not only have they created, cherished and protected champagne, but they have also created, cherished and protected something that, subsequently, has been every bit as important as the wine itself: its image.

Indeed one of the few reproaches one can make to the champagne producers is that they have succeeded too well in their image-building. Champagne can seem a little haughty and forbidding to newcomers, a little too exclusive and nobby, perhaps a little too far removed from the soil and the labour of the winegrower, and certainly too expensive. Attempts to 'democratize' champagne have been half-hearted, as if the producers suspected that, in doing this, they might begin to pull down the edifice so carefully erected over so many years.

Yet a democratization has taken place, via the growth in sales of 'own-brand' champagnes and growers' champagnes. The latter, in particular, are likely to be seen outside France more often in the future, while the *grandes marques* (the leading champagne companies) will specialize increasingly in top-quality wines sold throughout the world. The image of champagne is unlikely to alter in substance in the years to come – it will remain the first and foremost of sparkling wines – but it may broaden and diversify thanks to these trends.

The cool, chalky slopes of the Champagne region in north-east France proved ideal for the production of the world's most famous sparkling wine.

THE LANGUAGE OF CHAMPAGNE

Appellation *Appellation d'origine contrôlée* (AC). Legal designation guaranteeing a wine by geographical origin, grape variety and production method. Champagne is the only *appellation* wine which does not state the AC formula on its label.

Assemblage Blending of still wines from different villages and, often, years to create a *cuvée* or blend, ready for bottling and second fermentation. Also one of two methods used to colour rosé champagne: still red wine is blended with white to produce the desired colour. See also *maceration*.

Autolysis Enzymatic breakdown of dead yeast cells. This takes place in the wine after the second fermentation; it gives complexity of flavour.

Balthazar Large bottle containing 12 litres, equivalent to 16 standard bottles.

Blanc de Blancs Champagne made only from white grapes.

Blanc de Noirs Champagne made only from black grapes.

Brut Dry champagne, containing not more than 15 grams per litre of residual sugar.

BOB See *own label*.

CIVC Comité Interprofessionnel du Vin de Champagne, co-ordinating body which regulates grape growing and wine production in Champagne.

CM *Coopérative de manipulation*. This code appears on labels of co-operative-produced champagnes.

Crémant Style of champagne with a less vigorous sparkle than normal. From September 1994, this term will no longer be applicable to champagne, but will be used for sparkling wines from other parts of France.

Cru Literally 'growth', used to signify the vineyards of a village. See also *premier cru, grand cru*.

Cuvée First 2050 litres of juice pressed from each 4000kg of grapes – the highest-quality juice. Also a finished blend, usually a combination of many *crus*.

Cuvée de prestige Top-of-the-range wine usually vintage-dated, always expensive.

Dégorgement Removal from the bottle of yeast sediment, left after the second fermentation; usually now done *à la glace*, by freezing the neck of the upended bottle so that the sediment forms an icy plug which can then be easily ejected.

Demi-sec Sweet champagne, containing between 33 and 50 grams of residual sugar per litre.

Deuxième taille Final 206 litres of juice that may be pressed from each 4000kg of grapes. Less fine in quality than the *cuvée* and *première taille*, it is used for cheaper, and sweeter, champagnes.

Dosage Amount of sugar added to finished champagne in the *liqueur d'expédition*; it governs final sweetness.

Dry/Sec Medium-sweet champagne, containing between 17 and 35 grams of residual sugar per litre.

Échelle des crus Literally 'ladder of growths'. Quality classification system, on a percentage point basis, of the 250 villages in the Champagne region. See also *cru, grand cru, premier cru*.

Extra Dry/Extra Sec Medium-dry champagne, containing between 12 and 20 grams of residual sugar per litre.

Grand cru Village rated at 100 per cent on the *échelle des crus*; champagne made entirely from grapes grown in these villages may be labelled *grand cru*.

Grande marque Term describing the largest and most important champagne houses.

Jereboam Large bottle containing three litres, equivalent to four standard bottles; also known as a double magnum.

Lattes Wooden slats used to separate layers of bottles during, and after, the second fermentation. During *sur lattes* ageing the wines acquire depth and complexity from contact with the second fermentation lees.

Lees Coarse sediment, such as dead yeasts, deposited by a wine after fermentation (first and second).

Liqueur d'expédition Solution of sugar and wine added to champagne after *dégorgement*. See also *dosage*.

Liqueur de tirage Solution of sugar, wine and yeast added to the finished blend when it is bottled, in order to provoke a second fermentation.

MA *Marque d'acheteur*. This code on a champagne label indicates that the name on the label is not the producer's but one chosen by the seller of the wine. Such wines are known in the UK as BOB (buyer's own brand) or 'own-label', and as 'private label' in the USA.

Maceration One of two techniques used to colour rosé champagne. It involves steeping a part of the Pinot Noir or Meunier juice with the skins to leach out colour. See also *assemblage*.

Magnum Double-sized bottle containing 1.5 litres. The best size for champagne that is to be aged for a long period.

Malolactic fermentation Not a true fermentation, but a bacteriological conversion of malic acid into lactic acid (and carbon dioxide), lowering the total acidity of a wine.

Marc The capacity of a champagne press, equivalent to 4000kg of grapes. Also the debris of pips, skins and stalks left after pressing; and the spirit distilled from this debris.

Methusalem Large bottle containing six litres, equivalent to eight standard bottles.

Millésimé See *vintage champagne*.

Mousse Froth of bubbles that results from the second fermentation in bottle.

Must Newly-pressed grape juice which is ready for fermentation to begin.

Nebuchadnezzar Large bottle containing 15 litres, equivalent to 20 standard bottles.

NM *Négociant-manipulant*. Signifies that the wine is produced by the champagne house named on the label.

Non millésimé See *non-vintage*.

Non-vintage (NV) Champagne blended from several years and sold without a vintage date. Known in French as *non millésimé* or *sans année*.

Own label Common English term for a BOB or MA-coded champagne – one labelled with the name of the seller (or one chosen by the seller) rather than that of the producer.

Premier cru Village rated at between 90 and 99 per cent on the *échelle des crus*; champagne made entirely from grapes grown in such villages may be labelled *premier cru*.

Première taille Second portion of juice (410 litres) pressed from each 4000kg of grapes. The *première taille* follows the *cuvée* and precedes the *deuxième taille*.

Prise de mousse Process whereby champagne acquires its sparkle; it takes place slowly during the second fermentation, inside the bottle.

Pupitre Two hinged boards containing 60 angled holes each, used for holding the bottles during *remuage*.

Racking Transferring wine from one container to another, to separate it from its lees.

RC *Récoltant-coopérateur*. Indicates a champagne made by a co-operative, but sold by a grower who belongs to that co-op.

Rehoboam Large bottle containing 4.5 litres, equivalent to six standard bottles; also known as a triple magnum.

Remuage Riddling. The twisting, jolting and gradual inversion of bottles in *pupitres*; the aim is to gather the second fermentation deposits in the neck, ready for *dégorgement*.

Remueur Worker charged exclusively with *remuage*.

Reserve wines Still wines of a particular vintage set aside and stored. They are used for blending in subsequent years.

RM *Récoltant-manipulant*. This code indicates champagne made by a grower, as opposed to a large champagne house or a co-operative.

Salmanazar Large bottle containing nine litres, equivalent to 12 standard bottles.

Sans année See *non-vintage*.

Sec See *dry*.

Second fermentation Fermentation, provoked by the sugar and yeast in the *liqueur de tirage*, that takes place inside the bottle. It causes the wine to acquire a sparkle.

SR *Société de récoltants*. Signifies that the wine was made by a family company of winegrowers.

Vintage champagne Champagne made from the wine of a single, good-quality year. Also known as millésimé.

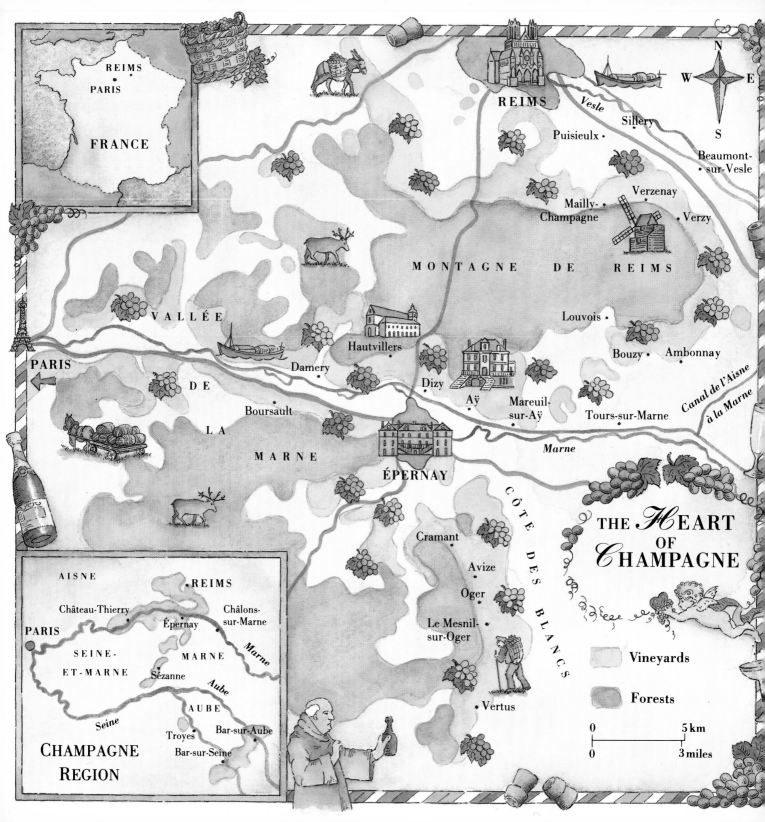

REIMS
PARIS

FRANCE

REIMS

Vesle

Sillery

Puisieulx •

Beaumont-
sur-Vesle

Verzenay

Mailly-
Champagne •

Verzy

MONTAGNE   DE   REIMS

Louvois •

Bouzy •   Ambonnay

VALLÉE

Hautvillers

Damery •

DE

Dizy •

LA

Aÿ •   Mareuil-
sur-Aÿ

Tours-sur-Marne

Canal de l'Aisne

à la Marne

PARIS

Boursault

MARNE

Marne

ÉPERNAY

Cramant •

Avize •

Oger •

Le Mesnil-
sur-Oger

CÔTE DES BLANCS

THE *H*EART
OF
*C*HAMPAGNE

Vertus •

Vineyards

Forests

0   5 km

0   3 miles

AISNE

REIMS

Château-Thierry •

Châlons-
sur-Marne

PARIS

Épernay

Marne

SEINE-

MARNE

ET-MARNE

Sézanne •

Aube

AUBE

Seine

Troyes •

Bar-sur-Aube

Bar-sur-Seine

CHAMPAGNE
REGION

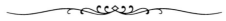

Traditionally, remuage *is done on these hinged boards or* pupitres, *developed by widow Clicquot using her kitchen table. These* pupitres *are in Perrier-Jouët's cellars.*

The widow's table

Dom Pérignon's method of storing the bottles upside down in sand was an imperfect process: the yeast deposits, or lees, contain sticky materials, and these often cling to the sides of the bottles while the rest of the sediment falls. What was needed was a gradual inversion – and a little jolt every now and again to shift those clinging lees. This was one of the first problems Nicole-Barbe Clicquot, newly widowed, turned her mind to in 1806 on assuming control of her late husband's company. She set to work, so the story goes, on her kitchen table, instructing cellarmen to drill bottle-neck-sized holes in it. Bottles were then inserted in the holes, where they could be twisted sharply at intervals. Her cellarmaster, Antoine Müller, hit on the refinement that provided the perfect solution: cutting the holes at a 45° angle. This meant that the bottles could be placed in the holes almost horizontally – the position in which they had acquired their sparkle – and gradually moved up to

the vertical, a twist and jolt at a time. By 1850, the use of boards with angled holes – now called *pupitres* – had become standard practice for all companies.

Workers in iron masks

The other problem requiring urgent solution was that of the exploding bottle. July and August were the most dangerous months: the second fermentation was then at its height, the warmth of summer was in the air, at least in the shallower galleries – and the cellarmen wore iron masks. In 1828, a particularly trying year, there was an explosion rate of 80 per cent. It was heart-breaking to see so much work come to nothing, and heart-stopping to see so much capital reduce itself to broken glass and gutter wine. The root cause was that the process of refermenting inside the bottles was mastered in outline but not in detail. It was those details that made all the difference between shattered glass in the cellar and an intact and deliciously foaming bottle on the customer's dinner table.

Antoine François, a chemist from Châlons-sur-Marne, took an important step towards overcoming the problem in 1836, when he invented the *sucre-oenomètre* – a device for measuring the levels of sugar left in the base wine before secondary fermentation. From this, he drew up tables indicating the amount of sugar that should be added to pro-

Breakages are now rare, and are today usually due to a fault in the glass.

duce different pressures of sparkle in the wines giving the winemakers more control. At the same time, glass manufacturers developed stronger bottles. Breakages were down to eight per cent by 1842; today the breakage rate is less than five bottles per thousand.

SALESMEN ADVENTURERS

THE TECHNICAL ADVANCES of the nineteenth century were a great help to the salesmen who travelled the world promoting champagne. One of the boldest was Veuve Clicquot's Monsieur Bohne, a stocky German Jew with a vivid letter-writing style. In his early days with widow Clicquot, he often complained about the quality of her wines. But by 1814, enthusiasm had replaced displeasure. 'It is with indescribable satisfaction' he wrote, 'that I have examined the samples. Spring water is infinitely less limpid than they are. Every palate in town is avid to taste them ... I had only to let drop the number of my hotel room, and a queue formed outside my door.' He was in Königsberg, near the Russian border, as part of a canny plan he had concocted with the Veuve to evade a Russian embargo of French goods. Luck was on their side: while Bohne was on his way to Königsberg the embargo was lifted, and within a month Clicquot champagne was all the rage in St Petersburg.

Charles-Camille Heidsieck, the original 'Champagne Charlie'.

Imperial custom

Two other houses, Charles Heidsieck and Roederer, also exploited the Russian market. Imagine a young, fur-swathed Frenchman on a sturdy white horse, riding slowly through a birch grove in which the last snows of winter are lingering. Behind him rides his servant, and behind the servant a small train of champagne-laden packhorses. This was the 21-year-old Charles-Henri Heidsieck, journeying with his wines all the way to the banks of the Volga. Eighty years later this most exotic of travelling salesmen was still remembered in Russia.

Some of the greatest Russian successes of all, meanwhile, were realized on Roederer's behalf by a Monsieur Krafft, who succeeded in placing bottles of Roederer champagne on the Tsar's table. They stayed there as long as the Tsar did, thanks, at least in part, to the distinctive punt-less crystal glass bottle created by Roederer exclusively for their imperial client.

Mercier's magnificent cask of Hungarian oak complete with carvings by Henri Navlet.

The barman's arrest

Russia was not champagne's only large overseas market. America was another, and here the name of Charles-Camille Heidsieck, the son of Charles-Henri, is famous.

Charles-Camille made a number of visits to America, and won many friends and customers – and the nickname 'Champagne Charlie' – with his fearless and stylish salesmanship. In 1862, however, his luck ran out. It was the American Civil War that brought him across the Atlantic on this occasion – to defend his stocks and his carefully cultivated markets (he was selling 75,000 bottles a year in New Orleans alone). In order to make the final leg of his journey, he acted as barman on a boat travelling from Alabama to New Orleans, carrying in his luggage a diplomatic bag from the French consul in the former city to his counterpart in the latter. The bag contained a French government offer of textile provisions to the Confederate armies of the South. New Orleans, however, had fallen to the Yankees; the barman's bag was examined; the barman was arrested and imprisoned in Fort Jackson. It took four months to release him.

This was not the only setback he suffered in 1862. Having received several large payments from an American agent, he decided to invest in two ships loaded with cheap cotton on which he hoped to make a handsome profit back in France. Both vessels were intercepted by the Northern forces and destroyed. Meanwhile his agent David Bayaud, who owed him substantial sums, went bankrupt. 'Champagne Charlie' accepted that fortune was against him. He headed for home and near ruin.

There was, however, a happy postscript. A brother of the bankrupted agent, Thomas Bayaud, had made a fortune out of property deals in Denver. Thomas remembered the money owed by his brother to Charles-Camille, a man whom he had always admired, and his will revealed that he had made the latter his sole heir. A missionary brought the news back to an astonished 'Champagne Charlie', nine years after the original loss.

Barrels and balloons

The domestic market was not ignored by the champagne salesmen. To this day, Mercier is one of the leading brands in France, and this success has nineteenth-century roots. Eugène Mercier built his sales on a series of spectacular publicity coups, such as those he arranged for the Universal Exhibitions of 1889 and 1900. Mercier had a huge barrel built for blending (and display) purposes and he decided that the giant cask would be perfect for the 1889 Exhibition; so he put four wheels on the tun's cradle, knocked a hole in the cellar wall, and had the tun towed to Paris by 24 white oxen. The journey took three weeks, and reached its climax when an axle broke in Rue Lafayette in Paris, stranding the convoy there for a week, which was just the kind of publicity-generating accident that Mercier had the knack of attracting. In 1900, he tethered a balloon on the Champ de Mars, and offered tastings on board. A wind got up; the mooring broke; off went the balloon with a cargo of nine drinkers, a waiter and a case of Mercier champagne. It floated south-east, making stately progress for 16

Mercier's balloon caused a sensation at the 1900 Exhibition when it broke loose.

hours before coming to rest in German Alsace, without cost to life or limb. Mercier himself was fined 20 marks for illegally importing six bottles of champagne – and he gleefully paid up, to the sound of reporters' pencils scribbling.

HARD TIMES

THE TWENTIETH CENTURY HAS BEEN a golden age, and a dark age, for champagne. By the early 1900s, champagne had established itself as the cosmopolitan accompaniment to high living, appreciated around the world and turning heads wherever it went. But this success brought problems.

Fraud

In Champagne, few people would agree that there is anything sincere or even flattering in imitation. There was nothing but cynical greed in many of the imitations that sprang up throughout the nineteenth century. Wherever wine was produced, 'champagne' was produced – often by pumping gas into cheap white wine.

To defend the interests of champagne, producers got together and formed a *syndicat* (association) in 1882, and another similar grouping in 1912. Since 1941, protective work of this nature has been undertaken by the Comité Interprofessionnel du Vin de Champagne (CIVC), an organization which acts on behalf of both grape growers and wine producers. It has had great success within Europe, but less elsewhere: non-French 'champagne' is still on sale in the USA and Australia.

The phylloxera plague

There were problems in the heart of Champagne, too. One was phylloxera, the tiny, root-eating aphid that came from America in the 1860s and slowly laid waste to European vineyards. Champagne was luckier than most. Its first vineyard was not attacked until 1892, and by then, the 'cure' – grafting European vines on to American vine rootstocks – had been known for a decade or so. The arrival of phylloxera nevertheless caused consternation in the region because of the enormous expense entailed in defeating the insect. Effectively, every grower had to begin again from scratch. In addition to the cost of uprooting the old vines and planting new, grafted ones, there were four years with no income while the grower waited for the vines to reach maturity. The process of grafting was still underway when World War One broke out.

Internal strife

Before Europe's armies met in Champagne, the region lived through a conflict of its own. Champagne's successes not only attracted worldwide imitation, but also meant that vines were planted more and more extensively in Champagne itself, often in areas where they had never previously been planted – in Aisne and Aube. Some of the large merchants took to buying base wines from still further afield: one reputable house bought

In 1911, the growers' anger at hasty, unfair champagne laws erupted into violent riots.

In the ferocious destruction of World War One, buildings suffered, too. This was Moët's main entrance in 1918.

from Chablis; less scrupulous rivals bought from the Midi. Regulations were needed; a crisis was on its way.

In 1908, legislation had been passed ruling that certain communes in Marne and Aisne alone had the right to call their wines 'champagne'. The law, however, was weakly enforced. Under pressure from growers, tougher laws were passed on 11 February 1911.

The Aube growers, realizing that their champagne days were over, responded angrily. Thirty-six mayors resigned; 8000 growers marched through Bar-sur-Aube; an effigy of the prime minister was burned. The government backed down. When the Marne

In July 1918, Allied commander Marshal Foch launched an operation on the Marne which led to Germany's defeat.

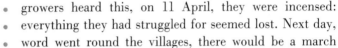

growers heard this, on 11 April, they were incensed: everything they had struggled for seemed lost. Next day, word went round the villages, there would be a march on Épernay.

The government had anticipated trouble and dispatched over 20,000 soldiers to the region. A squadron of cavalry blocked the road to Épernay; the marchers then headed for Aÿ, where the presence of a smaller squadron acted as an irritant rather than a deterrent. Forty-one buildings and warehouses were either ransacked or burnt; the gutters ran with wine; flames danced in the glitter of broken glass. The government set about producing a new law. This legislation was still before parliament when the German army entered Reims, on 3 September 1914.

The Champagne battlefield

Ten days later Reims was French again, but those ten days had seen terrible fighting all over Champagne's greatest vineyards, laden with the fruit of the 1914 harvest. The front line became fixed just north of Reims, and hardly moved in four years. Bombardments began on 14 September; five days later, Reims cathedral was burning so fiercely that the bells melted and the roof lead rained down.

Amazingly, champagne production continued during the war. As the men were fighting, most of the work was done by women, the old and the young. During the 1914 harvest, over 20 children died.

Clicquot's Hôtel de Marc has World War One scars.

WORLD WAR TWO

AFTER 1918, THE OUTLOOK FOR CHAMPAGNE continued gloomy. Many of the vineyards were ruined; many more had still to be grafted; the lucrative Russian market had disappeared; sales to Scandinavia slumped as prohibition was contemplated, and sales to America ceased almost completely when prohibition became law in 1920. *Almost* completely; the bootleggers ensured that champagne was always obtainable – even if it had been dumped on sandbanks, perhaps covered by a tide or two, and sold, label-less, for a mobster's ransom.

Prohibition lasted for 13 years; its repeal in 1933 was a cause for celebration both in the USA and in Champagne, which welcomed the return of a major market for its wines.

Meanwhile, champagne legislation had again become an issue; in 1927 new laws replaced those that were being passed in 1914, and the vineyards of the Aube were readmitted to the circle of the elect. Stocks grew. And sales dwindled: the British market, which had held up well in the post-war years, slowed markedly during the Great Depression. The only real success of the 1930s for champagne was a threefold increase in French sales.

Occupation

World War Two saw less spectacular damage done to the region than in 1914–18, but the period was a traumatic one nonetheless.

The region was undefended militarily, and Reims was in German hands by May 1940. Otto Kläbisch, a Rhine wine merchant, was made Director of the Reims office co-ordinating supplies to Germany, and he issued orders outlining the future of champagne: civilians would no longer be entitled to the wine without special authorization; every three weeks, one million bottles were to be sent to the German armed forces.

How could the champagne-makers fight back? Commercial disobedience on a large scale was impossible, but many firms and growers worked to ensure that small-scale disruptions were common occurrences; as a result, Kläbisch found his job was far from easy. It was this situation that gave rise to the one positive development during World War Two in Champagne: the formation of the CIVC – initially a liaison body between the German authorities and the champagne industry. Comte Robert-Jean de Vogüé of Moët & Chandon worked for the CIVC on behalf of the champagne houses, while Maurice Doyard represented the growers.

Dark days

The CIVC had some successes – permission to sell one-quarter of production to civilians in France, Belgium, Sweden and Finland; and the non-deportation of young men from Reims on the grounds that they were needed

An advert for champagne from the post-war years when sales began to soar.

to work in the cellars — but thereafter relations between it and the authorities deteriorated. In 1942, de Vogüé and his assistant were condemned to death for being 'destructive'; but in the face of mass protest, their sentences were commuted to imprisonment. They were deported and spent the rest of the war in concentration camps.

Another war hero was the Marquis de Suarez d'Aulan of Piper-Heidsieck, an active resistance member who used the firm's cellars as a store for arms parachuted in by the Allies. The Germans found out, but d'Aulan was able to get away to Spain — where Franco imprisoned him. He bribed his way out of jail, made for Algeria, there joined the Lafayette Thunderbolt Squadron and flew a number of missions before losing his life over Mulhouse. Piper-Heidsieck, meanwhile, was sequestrated. So was Moët & Chandon, home to another resistance cell. A number of Moët's senior staff were deported; four never returned.

The invaders left rapidly, towards the end of August 1944. General Patton's 3rd Army arrived on the 28th. Rumour had it that the Germans intended blowing up many of Champagne's cellars before they went, but the speed of the American advance took them by surprise.

Return to the sunlight

The post-war history of champagne has been almost shockingly successful. When the champagne-makers began to piece together the broken fragments of trade after 1944, they had little reason to be optimistic. Considerable amounts of wine had been lost to the Germans; the vineyards had been ill-maintained; above all, they had been severed from their vital foreign markets, many of which had changed politically. Stalin now laid claim to much of Eastern and Central Europe, while in Western Europe, socialism was a rising political force. It was not easy to see a role for champagne in such an austere and egalitarian future.

Good wine, however, has proved more attractive than political theory. In 1949, 28 million bottles of champagne were sold; by 1989, that figure had increased almost tenfold, to 248 million bottles. In 1949, about 11,500 hectares (28,416 acres) were in production; at the beginning of 1989, the figure had more than doubled, with further vineyards planted. Champagne, indeed, can now expand no further.

New vines on the Montagne de Reims. Almost all of Champagne's 35,000 hectares (84,484 acres) are now planted, making further expansion impossible.

SECRETS OF THE CHAMPAGNE METHOD

There are few wines as complicated to make as champagne. At certain stages of its life it needs to be left alone, and at others it needs to be fussed over. It is blended, twice fermented, and has sticky lees that must be removed from inside the bottle without letting its precious sparkle escape.

The stratagems for overcoming these problems are varied and ingenious, the fruit of several hundred years spent in the pursuit of perfection. Collectively, these solutions and techniques are known as the champagne method – the famous *méthode champenoise*. The end result is the finest sparkling wine in the world.

The light glows through this bank of inverted bottles of Belle Époque Rosé awaiting remuage *– one of the complex processes that make up the painstaking* méthode champenoise.

VINES AND GRAPES

IN THE PUREST SENSE, THERE IS NOTHING SECRET about the champagne method: it is widely studied and imitated throughout the wine-growing world for the creation of sparkling wines. Yet nowhere else in the world is the method practised with such scrupulous care, nor does anywhere else enjoy Champagne's natural advantages for making wines in this way. As a consequence, champagne reigns supreme among sparkling wines.

The Moulin de Verzenay, on the Montagne de Reims, is Champagne's only windmill. Built in 1820, it now belongs to Heidsieck-Monopole. Verzenay is a grand cru *village.*

Cool chalklands

Champagne's natural advantages begin in the vineyards, on the rolling chalky slopes that rise up graciously from the beet fields of the plain. The gentle hillsides provide good drainage and exposure for the vines, and the chalky subsoils yield light, delicate wines. Chalk, how-

ever, is such an austere medium that the vines would fall sick with a deficiency-related disease called chlorosis if it weren't for the topsoils; these are much richer in organic matter than the chalk subsoils and so act as a nourishing stockpot for the plants. To do this, they, in turn, need constant replenishment: with modern fertilizers; with the lignite-rich, peaty *cendres noires* (black cinders) quarried from the Montagne de Reims; and – surprisingly but successfully – with finely shredded town refuse, eye-catching for the scraps of blue plastic it contains.

As a protection against early spring frosts, the vines are sprayed with water; ice then forms and insulates the young, vulnerable buds.

Champagne's cool climate also plays a vital part in the success of its vines. This is the most northerly of France's vineyards, and its 1537 hours of sunshine per year are only just enough to ripen grapes. Such a marginal climate poses many problems for growers: winter frosts can be so severe as to kill vines, and spring frosts can destroy fruitful buds; May and June rains can wash pollen from the flowers, while July and August rains can set mildew and rot among the grapes; crop-shattering hail is likely at any time; and, in some years, there just isn't enough sunshine to get sugar levels in the grapes up to an acceptable level. Yet the risks are worth running because the nervy, flowery, markedly acidic wines that are produced when all goes well make the perfect base materials for the world's finest sparkling wine.

Grape talk

Three grape varieties are used in Champagne today: the Chardonnay, Pinot Meunier and Pinot Noir. Each of these varieties occupies about one-third of the total vineyard area, and each is grown in distinct zones: Pinot Noir dominates on the Montagne de Reims, particularly in its south-western sector, and in the Aube; Pinot Meunier dominates in the Vallée de la Marne and in the Aisne; while Chardonnay dominates on the Côte des Blancs. Pinot Meunier and Pinot Noir are both black grape varieties, while Chardonnay is white. Most non-vintage champagne is a blend of wines from all three varieties, for each has a contribution to make. Chardonnay produces light, fine and flowery wines, with a lively, crisp-apple acidity; Pinot Noir adds body, depth of flavour and fullness; while Pinot Meunier provides aromatic sweetness, a lush fruitiness and the capacity to acquire the roundness of age comparatively rapidly.

Chardonnay and Pinot Noir are the varieties planted in most *grand cru* and *premier cru* sites. The terms *grand* and *premier cru* refer to the vineyards of a number of especially well-positioned villages. All 250 villages in the champagne *appellation* zone are classified by a system known as the *échelle des crus* (literally 'ladder of growths'). Within this system, the vineyards of the best villages are given a rating of 100 per cent, and the worst 80 per cent; most lie somewhere in between. The 'per cent' refers to the 'official' price of a kilo of grapes as recommended each year by the CIVC (Comité Interprofessionnel du Vin de Champagne). Grapes from villages classified at 80 per cent command, in theory, only 80 per cent of the decreed price per kilo, while those from

In the vineyard this mobile incinerator burns vine prunings as they are cut. At the same time, it provides welcome warmth, and produces ash to help fertilize the soil.

vineyards in 100-per-cent-rated villages command the full price. Any village enjoying a classification of 90 to 99 per cent may call itself a *premier cru*; those with a 100 per cent classification are *grands crus*.

Black and white

But how can you make a white wine from black grapes? Anyone who has ever gone to the trouble of peeling and seeding grapes for an elaborate fruit salad will know that the pulpy flesh inside black grapes looks identical to that inside white grapes. The flesh is light green, and the juice is colourless; all the red-black colour lies in the skins. By pressing black grapes very gently, therefore, so that the juice isn't stained by the skins, a white wine can be obtained. In fact the juice is light pink as it runs from the presses, but this colour drops away as the juice settles and then ferments.

Chardonnay (left) and Pinot Noir (right) are the two finest champagne grapes.

THE FIRST SIX MONTHS

THE CHAMPAGNE METHOD BEGINS with the pressing of the grapes, as for any white wine. But in Champagne, this is a closely controlled matter, with only 2666 litres of must – newly pressed juice – permitted from every 4000kg of grapes. Even those 2666 litres have to be extracted in three separate batches: the first 2050 litres are the best, and are known as the *cuvée*; the next 410 litres are called the *première taille*; and the final 206 litres, the *deuxième taille*. The grapes will yield more juice, but such juice may only be distilled; it cannot be used for champagne. A complete pressing cycle takes about four hours.

Sugar into alcohol

After pressing, the must is allowed to rest for 10 to 24 hours, so that any impurities and solids can settle out. It then undergoes its first fermentation, during which the sweet grape juice becomes dry wine.

Gosset's cellarmaster checks the vat temperature. Gosset uses a range of containers for fermentation: wooden casks, cement tanks, tile-lined tanks and stainless-steel vats.

Mumm uses wooden presses for its Chardonnay crop. Traditional presses like these are still common throughout Champagne, even though modern alternatives are available.

Each gram of sugar in the juice is converted by the yeasts into equal quantities of alcohol and carbon dioxide, plus tiny amounts of other flavour-giving substances. Most companies carry out this first fermentation in large, stainless steel tanks, kept in cellar areas where the temperature is maintained at around 20°C. A few companies, such as Krug, Gratien and Bollinger, still use traditional 205-litre wooden casks for all or some of this alcoholic fermentation. If natural grape sugar levels are inadequate, the musts may be chaptalized – that is, have sugar added to them in order to increase their final alcohol content.

Following the turbulence of alcoholic fermentation, the wines rest for some months. During this time most of them undergo malolactic fermentation – not a true fermentation, but a bacteriological conversion of malic acid into lactic acid. In taste terms, the wines lose their sharp, green acidity and, while retaining their liveliness, become slightly smoother and fuller.

More rest follows during the dark winter months, after the malolactic fermentation has finished. Periodically the wines will be transferred from tank to tank, from cask to cask, to separate them from the yeast deposits left behind after fermentation. This is known as racking.

Tasting the future

In February, the most critical moment in the champagne producer's year arrives: *assemblage* or blending. This is when all the wines that a champagne maker wishes to use for a commercial blend – a *cuvée* – are brought together and bottled. It is a time of decision; once the wine is blended and bottled, there is no going back, and imperfections would haunt their perpetrator for years.

What makes the task particularly awesome is the work of imagination involved. The base wines are acid, loose-knit and unappealing. The blender must constantly think ahead: what will they taste like when charged with carbon dioxide gas, when slightly higher in alcohol, when a little sweeter, when further aged and enriched by the yeasty deposits of second fermentation?

All the blender has to go on are the successes and, perhaps, failures of the past; and even those may be difficult to interpret. Every year he starts anew. Take the example of cellarmaster Daniel Thibault at Charles Heidsieck. He uses wines from over 100 different villages in his Brut Réserve blend – not only wines from the latest vintage, but also reserve wines from older vintages which have been held back to add depth and texture. As he works, he must also think of what he needs for the company's other champagnes, and he has to think about setting up new reserve wines for future

use, too. It is rather like putting together a jigsaw puzzle when you have only a hazy idea of the final picture – and with all the pieces cut similarly, so that there is almost no limit to the number of ways in which you could proceed. Needless to say, the exact formula for an *assemblage* is always a closely kept secret.

A Krug worker racks still wine from one fermentation cask to another; racking separates the wine from its sediment.

Going underground

Once *assemblage* is complete, most houses cold-stabilize their wines – to get rid of harmless but unattractive tartrate crystals – and then bottle them. As the wines are bottled, they are dosed with *liqueur de tirage*. This mixture of young wine, 17 to 24 grams of sugar, and yeasts will induce a second fermentation. The bottles, sealed with a small, inverted plastic pot and crown cap, are then taken deep down into the cellars. Here they are stacked horizontally, each row separated from the next by *lattes* (thin strips of wood). They are piled perhaps 15 or 20 rows high, and up to 40 or 50 bottles deep. These massive banks, stretching away into the darkness like honeycombs of glass, make a haunting sight.

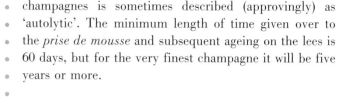
CAPTURING THE SPARKLE

IN THE CELLARS, A SECOND FERMENTATION takes place inside each bottle. The yeasts consume the sugars, raising the alcohol level by just over one per cent, and the pressure of dissolved carbon dioxide to between five and six atmospheres – a process known as the *prise de mousse* (capturing the sparkle). All this happens very, very slowly, as the temperature in these underground vaults is between 9°C and 12°C, rather than the 20°C or so at which the first fermentation takes place. The cooler the temperature, the more lazily the yeasts set about their work. This leisurely pace, however, is crucial, as it is thought to be one of the reasons why champagne has such deliciously petite bubbles, such fine creamy foam.

When all the sugar from the *liqueur de tirage* has been converted into gas and alcohol, the yeasts have nothing further to live on, so they die – and are deposited on the side of the bottle. Yet these deposits, the lees, still have important work to do, even in their dead state, for the wine acquires depth and complexity of flavour from their presence and their slow enzymatic break-down. This process of decomposition is known as autolysis, and is another key factor in champagne's superiority over other sparkling wines. Indeed, the flavour of certain champagnes is sometimes described (approvingly) as 'autolytic'. The minimum length of time given over to the *prise de mousse* and subsequent ageing on the lees is 60 days, but for the very finest champagne it will be five years or more.

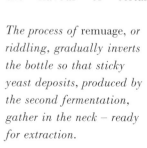

The process of remuage, *or* riddling, *gradually inverts the bottle so that sticky yeast deposits, produced by the second fermentation, gather in the neck – ready for extraction.*

Twist and turn

How to remove the soft and sticky lees from the bottle efficiently, without muddying the wine or losing its sparkle, must be the most teasingly difficult problem encountered in the champagne method. It is solved by a process known as *remuage*.

In order to eject the sediment cleanly, it must be gathered in the neck of the bottle. To achieve this, the bottles are 'riddled', traditionally in wooden *pupitres*, the hinged boards with angled holes developed by Veuve Clicquot. The bottles are placed in the holes almost horizontally, and are then gradually twisted and turned up to the vertical by quiet, pale men wearing thin cotton gloves. These are the *remueurs*, the bottle-riddlers, whose singular task in life is to move through the damp chalk caverns turning and jolting up to 50,000 bottles a day. This is skilled work, not just because of the speed of the operation, but also because there is a precise sequence of turns to and fro to be followed, each step being gauged by the position of a dab of chalk paste on the bottom of the bottle. *Remueurs*, for their speed and skill are the highest paid of Champagne's cellar workers.

Cellar sunflowers

There are machines called *gyropalettes* that can do this work as efficiently, if less picturesquely, than the *remueurs*. They generally take the form of large crates on stands. The bottles are stacked horizontally in the crates, and the machine is then programmed to shake and turn the whole crate at set intervals. The angle gradually changes, the bottle-filled crate resembling the seedy face of a sunflower as it turns slowly up towards the sky – hence *girasol*, the 'sunflower' nickname given

than non-vintage champagne; it may not be. It should, however, be more characterful, more striking, more demanding. It will be at least two years older than an NV, though this may not be obvious; indeed it may even seem raw and unpolished by contrast with an NV, since blending wines of different ages is the main method by which roundness is given to non-vintage blends. It is generally advisable to give recently released vintages at least six months' extra ageing. Only the better years are used for vintage champagne; 1984 and '87, for example, were not vintage years. 1982, '83 and '85 are all good vintages, and 1988, '89 and '90 seem set to follow. Although 1980, '81 and '86 were not uniformly good, some producers still felt they had wines of sufficient quality to merit the production of a vintage *cuvée*. Previous vintages of distinction include 1979, '76, '75, '69, '59, '52 and '47.

Rosé

Rosé champagne

Enthusiasm for rosé champagne has waxed and waned since 1777, the year in which Philippe Clicquot is said to have first marketed such a wine. (Initially, of course, all champagne was rosé – or at least light red. White and sparkling wines came later.) Rosé champagne is more fashion-sensitive than other types, but at present, interest is keen, and all major houses produce a rosé.

These may be made in one of two ways. The first is by macerating a proportion of the red grape skins in either the must or fermenting wine: the skins stain the must pink. The second and more popular method is to add a proportion of still red wine, often from Bouzy and other Montagne de Reims villages, to the blend at the *assemblage* stage, and then later to the *liqueur de tirage* and *liqueur d'expédition*. The second method is preferred by most houses because it allows a more precise control of colour, and it also permits a sizeable proportion of Chardonnay to be included in the blend if wished. Either method, however, can produce rosé champagne of quality. The tone and depth of colour, sweetness and fruitiness of rosé champagne all vary considerably from producer to producer.

Blanc de Blancs, Blanc de Noirs

The term Blanc de Blancs (white of whites) signifies a champagne made from white grapes only, that is from Chardonnay. Similarly, Blanc de Noirs (white of blacks) describes a champagne made exclusively from one or both of the black varieties – Pinots Noir and Meunier.

A Blanc de Blancs should have great delicacy and creamy finesse; it may, however, need three or four years to acquire these characteristics, tasting sharp and short in its youth. Its aromas, too, improve with age. Most Blanc de Blancs originate in the Côte des Blancs.

The less common Blanc de Noirs should be a firmly fruity wine, and is sometimes rather earthy in character. It is a full yellow in colour, and makes a better food partner than does a Blanc de Blancs.

SPECIALITIES, SPARKLING AND STILL

THE CHAMPAGNES DESCRIBED on the previous pages account for 95 per cent or more of all sales. But Champagne, like every wine-producing region, has its own distinctive specialities, sold in small quantities but with great pleasure and pride.

Crémant champagne

Crémant (creaming) champagne is less fully sparkling than ordinary champagne, having only 3.6 atmospheres of pressure instead of between five and six atmospheres. This difference is not as easy to detect, in either the glass or the mouth, as one might suppose; nevertheless a good *crémant* champagne will possess some of the palate-caressing texture, and pleasingly lacy structure, that its name suggests. The term *crémant*, however, has recently been relinquished by Champagne and given to fully sparkling wines in other regions of France (Alsace, Burgundy, the Loire). In return, winemakers in these areas – and other sparkling wine producers in the EC – have agreed not to use the term *méthode champenoise* (champagne method) any more. Some champagne houses continue to use the term *crémant*, but this is only permitted until 31 August 1994.

Cuvées de prestige

Cuvées de prestige, also known as de luxe champagnes or, simply, as 'specialities' (*cuvées spéciales*), are top-of-the-line champagnes. They should be intense and deep in flavour, generally vintage-dated, well aged, and of

Cuvées de prestige

Crémant

impeccable style and quality – to justify a price never less than twice that of the same company's non-vintage.

Moët & Chandon's Dom Pérignon, launched in 1937 with the 1921 vintage, was the first champagne to be deliberately marketed as a *Cuvée de prestige*, and Roederer's Cristal, originally produced for the Russian imperial court, made an ideal competitor once the blend had been reworked to take account of modern tastes. All of Krug's champagnes fall into this top category, while Perrier-Jouët's Belle Époque (Fleur de Champagne in the USA) and Taittinger's Comtes de Champagne have also succeeded in capturing the public's imagination. But aside from these names, the creation of *cuvées de prestige* has not been, in commercial terms, as successful as the producers may have hoped.

Are they worth the money? That depends on how rich you are. If you are not rich, non-vintage and vintage champagne offer much better value. If you are rich, these are among the finest champagnes money can buy.

Still wines

Still wines, the ancestors of champagne, continue to be produced in the region – but in small quantities, with intermittent success, and at a very high price. The *appellation* is Coteaux Champenois, the 'Champagne slopes', and it covers red, white and rosé wines. The whites are, with a few exceptions, simple, unexceptional Chardonnays, often thin and sharp; the rosés are rarely seen, and even more rarely have any depth of flavour; the Pinot Noir-based reds, however, are capable of greater excellence, though only once or twice a decade – when they acquire the flesh and fullness to match their rather bony fruit. Village and vineyard names sometimes appear on the labels.

A separate *appellation* exists for Pinot Noir-based rosé produced at Les Riceys in the Aube: Rosé des Riceys. It is deep in colour and, after a good vintage, has the vibrancy of flavour that puts it well ahead of most rosé from the Coteaux Champenois.

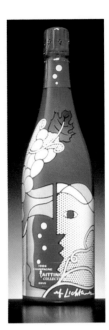

Taittinger Collection features superb vintages in spectacular bottles – created by artists like Victor Vasarely (left, 1978), Arman (centre, 1981) and Roy Lichtenstein (1985).

Ratafia and Marc

Ratafia is a local *mistelle*; in other words, grape juice fortified (and therefore prevented from fermenting) with strong local brandy. Red, rosé and white versions are both produced; the final strength varies from 18 to 23 per cent; levels of sweetness and length of cask ageing also vary from producer to producer.

Marc de Champagne is a spirit distilled from the grape skins, pips and stalks left behind after the juice has been pressed from the fruit. All *marc* has wild, savage flavours, and Champagne's is no exception, even after years of mellowing in oak casks: drink it with circumspection. There is also a local brandy distilled from wines that never qualified for the Champagne or Coteaux Champenois *appellations*; it is called Fine Marne, and the best examples have some of the lightness and verve of champagne itself.

DECODING THE LABEL

AFTER BEING CORKED, THE BOTTLES ARE LABELLED. Most of the information given on a champagne label is self-explanatory, covering basic details such as the producer's (or buyer's) name, address, degree of dryness, bottle contents and alcohol by volume. And, of course, there is the name of the wine itself, champagne – the only AC wine in France which does not require the full *appellation d'origine contrôlée* formula. The label also features the matriculation number – generally tucked away at the bottom and of significance only to a champagne official. This number is prefixed by two initials, indicating the status of the producer; the exact meaning of these various code letters is as follows:

NM – *négociant-manipulant*: champagne made by the house whose name appears on the label. All the large houses, such as Bollinger, Mercier and Mumm, sell under their own names, and these names act as an indicator of the quality and style of the wine in the bottle.

MA – *marque d'acheteur*: champagne blended to a buyer's specification; the name on the label is the buyer's (or distributor's), rather than the producer's. In the UK, these wines are known as BOB (buyer's own brand), and as 'private labels' in the USA. Supermarket 'own-label' champagnes belong to this category.

CM – *coopérative de manipulation*: champagne produced by a co-operative.

RM – *récoltant-manipulant*: champagne produced by a grower; it is RM rather than RC that is the true grower's code. This category is increasing in importance as more growers decide to make their own wine rather than supply grapes to the large houses.

RC – *récoltant-coopérateur*: champagne made by a co-operative, but sold by a grower who is a member of that co-operative. In practice, this means that there is little difference between the CM and RC codes.

SR – *société de récoltants*: champagne produced by a family company of wine growers.

The town where Pol Roger is based, one of the two most important centres for champagne.

A term to describe the style of champagne; although demi-sec *means medium dry, here it denotes a sweet wine.*

The word champagne must appear on labels to fulfil the appellation contrôlée *laws.*

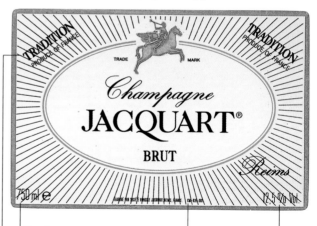

Bottle contents: 750ml (or 75cl) is the standard champagne bottle size. The 'e' is an EC guarantee of volume.

Alcoholic strength.

The brand used by Jacquart for its basic NV cuvée. Its premium NV cuvée is sold as Sélection.

The letters CM denote a wine made by a champagne co-operative.

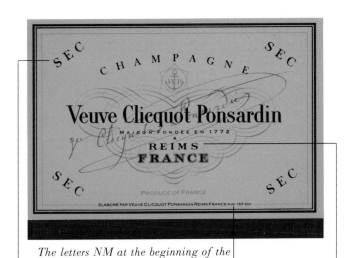

The letters NM at the beginning of the code denote the wine of the company named on the label.

The style of champagne; although sec means dry, it denotes a medium-sweet champagne.

The capital of the Champagne region; Veuve Clicquot is based here.

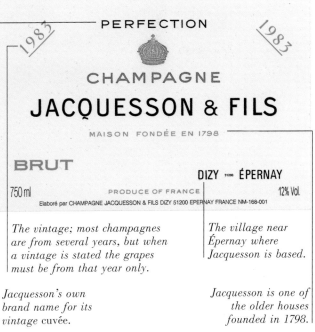

The vintage; most champagnes are from several years, but when a vintage is stated the grapes must be from that year only.

The village near Épernay where Jacquesson is based.

Jacquesson's own brand name for its vintage cuvée.

Jacquesson is one of the older houses founded in 1798.

The village in the Marne département where Vilmart is based.

The letters RM denote a champagne made by a grower.

The brand Vilmart uses for its premium NV cuvée.

The most popular style of champagne; brut means dry.

The name of the house appears on all labels.

The grape variety. All blanc de blancs champagnes are made only from Chardonnay grapes.

The name of Taittinger's cuvée de prestige.

A champagne made only from white grapes.

SELLING CHAMPAGNE

Champagne is unique in that, from its earliest
days, it has been a wine not only for local
consumption, but for the drinkers of the world.
Ingenuity and skill were needed to promote
champagne across oceans and borders and,
to this end, posters, labels and other publicity
materials were commissioned from leading
artists and illustrators of the day. The resulting
images are enticing, beautiful and frequently
witty. They make a powerful appeal in any
language, any country and at any time. Judge
for yourself from the selection reproduced on
the following pages.

*Continuing the great ballooning tradition begun by
Mercier in the 1800s, Moët & Chandon's giant cork floats
towards Japan's Mount Fuji.*

THE ART OF THE POSTER

CHAMPAGNE
JOSEPH PERRIER

Fantasy has played a major role in champagne advertising, as the producers urge their artists to find ways of convincing us that drinking champagne means escape from humdrum reality. This red-cheeked vineyard 'mermaid' dreamed up by Joseph Perrier's artist symbolizes the transformation of grapes into happiness – via the double magnum she cheerily waves.

CHAMPAGNE
HAU
&Cº
REIMS

- *Champagne Hau may no longer be with us, but Pre-Raphaelite illustrator Walter Crane's 1894 autumnal vineyard design seems likely to endure. Interestingly, most of the posters feature the coupe style of glass, which was the fashionable glass for drinking champagne in the nineteenth and early twentieth centuries. The tall, slender flute is now considered more suitable.*

Every age has its own
ephemera, and items like
these fans were as good a
way of spreading the word
in the twenties and thirties
as the ubiquitous tee-shirts
and carrier bags are today.
Modern designers, however,
would probably be asked to
increase the size of the
company name.

LABELS

A GLIMPSE OF SOME OF THE LABELS used in the past to identify bottles of champagne makes present-day examples, with a few distinguished exceptions, seem trite and tawdry. Bollinger's and Moët's mid-nineteenth century labels, and Veuve Clicquot's 1835 Sillery Mousseux (Sillery is a *grand cru* village sited next to Verzenay), leave the Moët 'American Independence' label looking a very poor and vulgar effort. Jacquesson and Ruinart (opposite) were two of the companies to persist with the traditional, intricate style of labelling well into the twentieth century, and Jacquesson does so to this very day. Ruinart has switched to modern labelling since its liaison with Moët & Chandon. Pol Roger has never abandoned classic simplicity in its label design, while Bruno Paillard uses paintings from his personal collection to illustrate his company's labels.

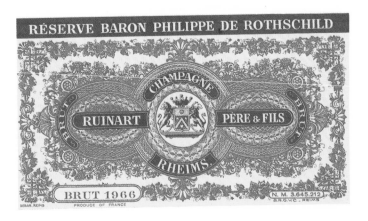

THE GREAT CHAMPAGNE HOUSES

Most champagne is made, not by vine growers, but by large companies who buy grapes or freshly pressed juice. Using these raw materials, and in conditions of high secrecy, they create a range of wines which they sell under their own names.

These are the great champagne houses, or *grandes marques*. Over the last two centuries or so, they have built the fortunes of this elegant wine worldwide. The profiles that follow give a flavour of some of the region's most celebrated names. Their stories, and the wines they create, differ greatly, and it is these differences which make champagne such an intriguing and enjoyable wine to discover.

The imposing façade of the headquarters at Aÿ of Bollinger, one of Champagne's most famous houses.

BOLLINGER

WIDOWS DOMINATE CHAMPAGNE'S HISTORY. Veuve Clicquot, Madame Pommery, Madame Krug, Camille Olry-Roederer . . . quite why champagne seems to be life-threatening for men, while bolstering resolve and longevity in women, is hard to say. Bollinger, too, owes much of its twentieth-century success to a widow: Madame Jacques, as she was known to her workers, and Tante Lily (Aunt Lily), as she was known to her family.

She was originally from Touraine, and was born Elisabeth de Lauriston, descendant of the eighteenth-century Scottish adventurer John Law of Lauriston. Her English governess used to call her 'Lily', and the name stuck. In 1923 she married Jacques Bollinger, the young 28-year-old head of the champagne house founded by his grand-father nearly a century earlier, in 1829. Jacques was a glamorous figure: he had been one of France's most distinguished airmen during World War One, and had been awarded the Légion d'Honneur, and the Croix de Guerre, before his twenty-fourth birthday.

Yet his health was not good. It was so poor by the outbreak of World War Two that he could no longer serve in the air force, and he died in 1941, aged only 47. The couple had no children. Madame Jacques took over, and she remained at the head of the company for 30 years.

She ran the company with a devotion and attention to detail that many of those who knew her attributed to her childlessness. It was as if Bollinger was the child she and Jacques never had.

Before Jacques died, she learned as much as was possible from him about the company, and soon put this knowledge to good use. She was a familiar figure in and around Aÿ – usually on her bicycle, which she rode almost to the end of her life. The length of her working day was legendary, as was her perfectionism – 'If I forgot something she had told me to do,' said her cellar-master, 'she had a voice and a face like iron'. She relaxed with embroidery and a stamp collection, while her only weakness was fierce brown cigarettes, rolled for her (and himself) by Jean Brunet, the head vineyard worker. Today the company is run by her nephew Christian Bizot.

The period during which Lily Bollinger was in charge, 1941–71, was a critical one, for it was then that many of the changes that has been made 'modern' champagne took place. Her position on these was conservative:

The small town of Aÿ, where Bollinger is based, known since medieval times for its high quality wines.

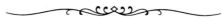

change nothing that would alter the Bollinger style. The result is that Bollinger remains a most traditional champagne.

What does this mean? It means that every wine the company makes (apart from the non-vintage) is from a single year, fermented in oak, and stored – often for a decade or more – on its second fermentation lees in a cork-stoppered bottle. It is impossible to be more traditional than that.

In taste terms, it means that Bollinger's champagnes have big, sweeping aromas and mouth-storming flavours, full of dry, toasty fruit and marked by the firm, 'winey' edge known as vinosity. They need age, and can be green and hard if drunk too young. If you are new to champagne, you may find them almost too challenging – but this is the true taste of champagne, and persistence will be rewarded.

Bollinger's position in Aÿ puts it in the middle of Champagne's greatest Pinot Noir vineyards so, as you might expect, Pinot Noir is the most important grape variety in all the company's blends. Special Cuvée is the Brut non-vintage, and Grande Année the vintage.

Bollinger's answer to the *cuvée de prestige* question is a typically traditional one: it releases a series of super-vintages, well aged (between eight and 15 years on the second fermentation deposits) and disgorged shortly before sale. The *dosages* are minimal; each is in the Extra Brut category, with less than six grams per litre of sugar. Fine vintages appear as RD (a Bollinger trademark, standing for Recently Disgorged); very fine vintages as Année Rare RD. These are wonderful, teasingly complex wines, and offer better value than the very rare and very expensive Vieilles Vignes Françaises, a pure Pinot Noir champagne produced from a small plot of pre-phylloxera vines behind the Bollinger offices. This wine was first produced to mark Lily Bollinger's seventieth birthday in 1969. It needs time to acquire its distinctive earthy richness – nearly as much time as we would need to save enough money to buy a bottle.

Madame Lily Bollinger used to visit the company's vineyards every day on her bicycle.

'I drink (champagne) when I am happy and when I am sad. Sometimes I drink it when I'm alone. When I have company I consider it obligatory. I trifle with it if I'm not hungry and drink it when I am. Otherwise I never touch it – unless I'm thirsty.'

LILY BOLLINGER

CHARLES HEIDSIECK

THE CHAMPAGNE CHARLIE REFERRED TO in the famous Victorian music-hall song, originally sung by George Leybourne, was Charles-Camille Heidsieck, the colourful and buccaneering owner of Charles Heidsieck. Unlike Louis Roederer and Veuve Clicquot, who concentrated on Russia, Charles-Camille targeted the British and American markets for his sales endeavours, and soon won something of a reputation in his own right – thanks to his shooting prowess. 'His love of sport is almost a mania,' wrote *Frank Leslie's Illustrated Newspaper* in January 1860. 'All the time which he can spare during the dull season of the wine trade he devotes to sport. The French papers state that for days he would ramble off from his estates, and venture into the swamps, morasses and woods for hundreds of miles, in the hope of discovering some new species of birds or animals to bring home as trophies.'

Sadly, this adventuring but perhaps foolhardy spirit nearly ruined the company when, during the American Civil War, Charles-Camille was imprisoned in a Mississippi fort for allegedly aiding the Confederate cause, his agent went bankrupt, and some cotton ships on which he hoped to make a handsome profit were fired and sunk all within a few months of each other.

During the twentieth century, the company has continued to have mixed fortunes. It was run by various members of the Heidsieck family, all of whom were called Charles-something or something-Charles, until 1976. The family worked hard but lacked both capital and vineyards, and the wines were inconsistent in quality. In 1976, it was taken over – though the move was described as a merger – by Henriot, another champagne house. Henriot invested in the company, giving it a splendid stainless-steel fermenting

The way I gained my title is a hobby
which I've got,
Of never letting others pay, however
long the shot.
Whoever drinks at my expense are treated
all the same;
From dukes and lords to cabmen down I make
them drink champagne.
Oh! Champagne Charlie is my name,
Champagne Charlie is my name...

'Champagne Charlie' was a huge success for George Leybourne in 1869 – but though the original Charlie was a Heidsieck, the words of the song, in fact, praised Moët's wines. The song's popularity caused many other performers to compose songs celebrating rival brands of champagne.

hall, but simultaneously depleted its stocks. In 1985, Charles Heidsieck became part of the Rémy-Martin (now Rémy-Cointreau group alongside Krug).

Since then, the company's champagnes have improved enormously, and its non-vintage Brut Réserve is now one of the best in its class and price bracket. Rémy told Charles Heidsieck's cellarmaster Daniel Thibault to 'make the blend you always wanted to make' for the Brut Réserve. To do this, Thibault set off on a wide-ranging search for fruit and now uses the wines of up to 120 different villages in the blend; he uses only the *cuvée* (first pressing); he also bought a large stock of reserve wines, incorporating up to 40 per cent of reserves in each new non-vintage *assemblage*; and he now ages the wines *sur lattes* for longer than before. Meanwhile, the bottles and labels were all redesigned, with lavish use of gold – always a good selling colour for champagne.

The result is that Brut Réserve (25 per cent Chardonnay, 37 per cent each Pinot Noir and Pinot Meunier) is now an extraordinarily vibrant wine, full of flowery apple and vanilla aromas and with a bright, dancing taste. It is a modern champagne in the best sense: clean and fresh, a product of stainless steel rather than seasoned oak, yet with the long complex flavours and fine, foamy bubbles that classic champagnes have always had. A Demi-Sec is also available.

The other wines in the Charles Heidsieck range are pretty good, too, though it is the Brut Réserve that offers the best value for money. The Vintage and the Rosé are, in effect, the same blend, save that 10-12 per cent still red wine is added to the Rosé. Both are big wines, with lots of lively fruit flavours.

The company's Blanc de Blancs and its prestige *cuvée* Champagne Charlie – a classic fifty-fifty mixture of Chardonnay and Pinot Noir – both ended with the 1982 vintage. They have been replaced by a prestige Blanc de Blancs called (with an eye to the year 2000) Blanc de Millénaire, 'millennium white'. The 1983 vintage has

Charles Heidsieck owns cellars in the crayères *area of Reims – chalk pits excavated by the Romans. Here cellarmaster Daniel Thibault inspects a bottle in one of these beautiful chalk vaults.*

flowery, nutty scents, suggesting macaroons after time in the glass; the flavour is dry, deep and cutting, more 'serious' in style than the rest of the range.

You may come across two other champagne companies with the name 'Heidsieck': Heidsieck-Monopole and Piper-Heidsieck. These two companies go back to one founder, Florens-Louis Heidsieck; they were formed after his death in 1828 by two nephews. Charles Heidsieck was founded still later, in 1851, Champagne Charlie being the son of a third nephew. All three companies have been independent of each other since their foundation – though Piper-Heidsieck has now also passed into the ownership of Rémy-Cointreau.

KRUG

THE ENTRANCE TO KRUG'S CELLARS lies off a quiet side-street in Reims. A cobbled courtyard faces you, and on three sides there are squat, sober-looking nineteenth-century buildings. They are well-maintained if unspectacular, and the place has a clean and tidy air. What would you guess it was? A small textile enterprise, perhaps, or a furniture depot? Unlikely as it may seem to the passer-by, it is the birthplace of the world's most expensive champagnes.

Krug's cellars have none of the extravagant grandeur of those of Moët & Chandon or Pommery; Krug's champagnes, though, are the grandest that money can buy. In terms of both cost and taste, all are in the *cuvée de prestige* category.

Four out of every five bottles of Krug are Grande Cuvée, a non-vintage – though winemaker Henri Krug prefers to call it a 'multi-vintage'. This is because wines from between six and nine different years find their way into the blend, which is a much wider range of reserves than most companies use. The result is a big, mouthfilling, super-complex champagne, one which really grips the tongue and leaves a taste of rich, dry fruit and a mineral-salty finish.

A Krug vintage is also produced, similar to the Grande Cuvée but less uniform in style. After particularly fine vintages, Krug keeps back stocks of its vintage champagne to age for many years more, releasing it eventually as part of the Krug Collection – a series of older vintages. Krug's rosé is a very pale, almost yellowy pink. Its full, leafy-strawberry scents give way to another very rich yet very dry taste, this time hinting at dewy Victoria plums.

Finally comes the world's most expensive champagne – Clos du Mesnil. This is a Blanc de Blancs produced uniquely from a small, walled vineyard inside the village of Le Mesnil-sur-Oger. The vineyard was bought by the company in 1971 and replanted; the first wine was from the 1979 vintage. Those who have tasted it speak admiringly of its delicate scent and rich, honeyed flavour – yet at around the same price as a London to New York air ticket, it offers value-for-money only to the very rich.

Far left *An aerial view of Krug's Clos du Mesnil (clos means 'walled vineyard'), birthplace of the world's most expensive champagne. The label, far right, shows the same scene.*

Left *Krug's cobbled courtyard in Reims in earlier times. Trucks have now replaced horses and carts.*

How is it that Krug manages always to make complex champagnes? One important factor is fermentation in wood. Originally, this was the way all producers made their champagnes, but nowadays most use big, stainless steel tanks. Krug still ferments every one of its wines in 205-litre wooden casks. This accentuates complexity of flavour rather than crispness and zinginess.

The second important factor is buying and blending, both the responsibility of Henri Krug. The company does not own many vineyards, but Henri is lucky enough to be able to afford to buy whatever and wherever he wants. So he buys small quantities of top-quality grapes from a very large number of villages, and carefully blends all the resulting wines together to produce the distinctive Krug taste. The wines are never filtered and are given at least six years' ageing on their lees before the *remuage*, thus adding further complexity.

This hunt for something that would lift the taste of a champagne beyond that of simple, well-made fizz goes back to the company's founder, Johann-Josef Krug. He was a German from Mainz, who had originally worked for the champagne house of Jacquesson. After nine years, despite family connections with Jacquesson, he decided to cut loose and set up on his own, and in 1843 he rented cellar space to do so. Before long, his wines were attracting attention and orders flowed in.

Johann-Josef – by now simply Joseph – was succeeded by his son Paul Krug, and he in turn by his oldest son Joseph II. During World War One, Joseph II was wounded and captured while fighting in the Ardennes; his wife Jeanne, in the best Champagne tradition, took over his duties. Indeed not only did she blend the wines and run the company successfully in his absence, but she also nursed in the local hospital and used the company cellars as a medical dispensary. Reims was under constant bombardment during this time, and no one was safe from the shells. Madame Krug herself was twice gassed, and was one of the last two women to leave the city in 1917. Her conduct during World War Two was

no less spirited: she helped stranded British and Canadian airmen find shelter and escape routes, and was twice imprisoned by the Gestapo as a result.

The company is run today by Henri and Rémi Krug, the grandsons of Joseph II and Madame Krug, and owned by Rémy-Cointreau. Henri is the one who stays at home, quietly going about the business of making and blending wines; Rémi, meanwhile, spends at least six months a year travelling the world, trying to convince customers, from Houston to Hong Kong,

Henri Krug, the master blender, working with still wines from the latest vintage.

that Krug is sufficiently special to warrant its high price. And, indeed, if any champagne can be worth ten times the price of an ordinary sparkling wine, then it is the majestic Krug Grande Cuvée.

LANSON

LANSON'S GREATEST SUCCESSES belong to the twentieth century – thanks to Black Label, the company's non-vintage champagne. Since its introduction, more than 50 years ago, Black Label has become one of the most familiar champagne names, second only to Moët & Chandon in certain markets.

The company developed out of one founded as far back as 1760, but it remained small until well into the nineteenth century. The first Lanson, Jean-Baptiste, created the name Lanson & Cie in 1837 and the current generation, Pierre and his brother Jean-Baptiste, is the sixth to work in the company. It was the energies and linguistic abilities of their grandfather Henri-Marie (as well as French, he was fluent in German, English and Dutch) that began Lanson's dramatic expansion. In 1919, his two sons Victor and Henri joined him, and from 1926 they began, much as Camille Olry-Roederer did, to buy vineyards at a time when it was unfashionable to do so. Over the years they assembled an attractive 192-hectare (474-acre) estate of vineyards spread among Champagne's most important villages.

The two brothers were also indefatigable globe-trotters. Henri, indeed, made America his base between 1935 and 1955, while Victor travelled almost everywhere else in the world. Between them, they set out to make the name of Lanson Black Label familiar to all. 'I make wine for myself. What I can't drink, I sell,' was Victor's professional creed. A legendary drinker, he set about proving it to customers over lengthy meals that would begin with a magnum of Black Label as an aperitif. 'He had a great head for figures, but he was a four-hour lunch man' remembers one British Lanson employee. One estimate puts the number of bottles of champagne drunk by Victor, during his 87 years, at 70,000.

Victor had ten children, six of whom followed him into the company. Today, Pierre and Jean-Baptiste continue to work for Lanson, although the family has not controlled the business since 1970. Sadly, in early 1991, a fourth change of ownership resulted in the loss of the substantial vineyard holdings which Victor and Henri had so carefully acquired. The new masters are Marne et Champagne, the own-label champagne specialists, acting in a joint venture with multinational Allied-Lyons. It is still too early to speculate on Lanson's future, but the major question is whether the quality of Black Label can be maintained without access to the old Lanson estate.

Despite the merry-go-round of owners, Lanson has succeeded in producing champagne of surprising consistency in recent years. The style is a very modern one: crisp, clean, bracing.

Stainless steel has replaced wood in Lanson's cellars – and improved the wines, according to Pierre Lanson.

The company doesn't have any wooden fermentation casks. 'We want champagne-tasting champagne, not wood-tasting champagne,' says Pierre Lanson. 'Wood was used in the past because we didn't have anything better; now we have stainless steel. I remember in the old days there used to be a room we called the infirmary, where we'd take all the casks which had a problem. We don't need an infirmary any more. Modern technology has brought us a lot. Controlling the fermentation temperature is one of the cornerstones of modern champagne production.'

Lanson is also the largest house to avoid malolactic fermentation systematically. 'Natural acidity is part of a champagne; it brings freshness. Drinkers are looking for acidity, though they don't like to admit it.' Avoiding the malolactic fermentation contributes fruity acidity to Lanson's champagnes, and that is perhaps the keynote to Black Label. Pierre Lanson, one of the team of six who decides on the *assemblage*, is not keen on the 'autolytic' or highly yeasty flavours of some old-school, super-traditional champagnes. 'When people say a champagne has nice, yeasty flavours, I say "Ugh!".'

Lanson is very proud of its vintage range; the aim is very definitely to respect the characteristics of the year, and the result therefore varies with each vintage. The general style is towards big, fruity wines with a firm backbone and a crisp finish. The non-vintage Rosé has a delicate, pale salmon colour with a taste that has the characteristic Lanson crispness, but is both long and pure. Lanson's *cuvée de prestige*, Noble Cuvée, is the most elegant and intense of the range, with a powdery lime-flower scent and a penetrating flavour.

Celebrating with champagne does not have to be a stiff, formal affair – that was the message of Lanson's 'why not?' series of advertisements. Black Label has a friendlier image than many of its rivals.

ℳERCIER

CHAMPAGNE FIRST CAME TO PROMINENCE, at the end of the eighteenth century, as a wine for the very, very wealthy. It was finnicky, time-consuming and labour-intensive to make; it needed expensive packaging; and one-third of the bottles exploded anyway before they reached the customer. Small wonder that early sales tours were a succession of court visits.

By the mid-nineteenth century, however, technical progress in the cellars and glass factories meant that champagne was no longer the preserve of crown princes and titled nobility. It was still expensive, and it remains so today, but for a treat or a special occasion, most of the growing middle classes could afford the occasional bottle. The democratization of champagne was underway.

The beaming, avuncular, walrus-moustached Eugène

Mercier did more than anyone else to bring champagne to the people. In 1858, when he was only 20, he found himself heading the Paris office of an association of five growers. He married the daughter of one of them, and soon transformed the association into a thriving company that bore his own name.

Mercier was never short of good ideas: he marketed a champagne in clear-glass bottles before Roederer; he registered the brand name Dom Pérignon before Moët (who subsequently acquired it via a marriage dowry); he built spectacular cellars in Épernay which were designed from the outset to be a tourist attraction; and he set about constructing what he hoped would be the largest barrel in the world.

To build a cask that would rival the Great Tun of Heidelberg was no easy matter: it took Eugène Mercier 20 years, and cost the lives of his two closest collaborators: the French cooper F Jolibois and the Hungarian cooper Heinrich Walter. Mercier went to Hungary with the aptly named Jolibois ('prettywood') and bought 250 centuries-old standing oaks; these mighty trees were felled over five autumns, and seasoned on the spot for a number more years.

Jolibois, in charge of constructing the cask, stayed in Hungary for two years as the timber was cut and shaped; bending the staves took a further seven years – each one was floated in Lake Balaton for 12 months before being heated, scalded and bent. This work was supervised by Walter, and it was in Balaton's reedy waters that he met his premature end.

Mercier took his cask, pulled by 24 oxen, to the 1889 Exhibition – and scored an unexpected publicity coup when the axle broke, stranding the convoy in a Paris street.

Eugène Mercier was a brilliant publicist.

The materials were ready in 1869, but – because of war – did not reach Épernay until 1874. The tun, its cradle, and the carvings by the cellar artist Navlet were officially completed on 7 July 1881, and on the same day Jolibois died, exhausted. On 8 July the names of F Jolibois and Heinrich Walter were branded inside the cask by Mercier.

The cask, a star turn at the 1889 Universal Exhibition, was just one of Mercier's publicity schemes. Balloons were another, and Mercier's offer of a glass of champagne on board a balloon for the celebration of the 1900 Paris Exhibition ended in an unscheduled flight to Alsace for nine drinkers, after a gust of wind broke the moorings.

Mercier maintains this airborne tradition today with its own stable of competition balloons – called Bulle d'Or (Golden Bubble) in France and Esprit d'Aventure (Spirit of Adventure) in Britain. The house continues to attract many visitors to Épernay.

Mercier's champagnes are among the cheapest of all those produced by the *grandes marques*. They are not great champagnes, nor do they claim to be. But they are better than they are often given credit for. The Brut is a good example of what the Pinot Meunier can produce when asked, with its sweet, appley scents and lush, ripe fruit. The Demi-Sec is soft and pretty, hinting at pears rather than apples. The Rosé has a rich *dosage* and creamy *mousse* to add charm to its strawberry fruit, while the Vintage is a little drier, yet still ripely peachy. Finally, visitors to France may encounter Bulle d'Or on shop shelves as well as gliding across the sky; this is Mercier's *cuvée de prestige*, sold only on the domestic market. Here the Chardonnay is more important than in Mercier's other blends, giving an elegant champagne.

France welcoming foreign nations to the Universal Exhibition of 1900 – with Mercier champagne, of course.

Bulle d'Or III ranges the skies, maintaining the Mercier tradition of high-profile, eye-catching publicity exploits.

MOËT & CHANDON

THE ABBEY OF HAUTVILLERS perches on the edge of the Montagne de Reims. Behind it lies thick forest; below stretch some of the most spectacular vineyards in Champagne. They form a great green amphitheatre, tumbling down towards the river Marne and Épernay. Dom Pérignon, Hautvillers' famous cellarer, knew this view as well as he did the sound of the abbey bell.

He would also have been familiar with the small village of Cumières. It is closer than any other to Hautvillers, lying almost directly beneath it on a lazy curve of the Marne. It was in this village, in 1683, that a boy called Claude Moët was born.

Moët inherited vineyards, and later in his life he traded as a wine merchant. The earliest of his account books to have been preserved for posterity is dated 1743, when the grower-merchant was 60, so that year is regarded as the founding date of the house. But since reference is made to earlier account books, business was clearly well under way by then. One of the first entries in the 1743 account book refers to a shipment down the Marne to Paris of 391 bottles for one of the French court's 12 official wine merchants, and by 1750 Madame de Pompadour, Louis XV's mistress, was a regular customer. The first export sale, to a Mr Gruppty of London, came in the same year.

It was Claude Moët's grandson, Jean-Rémy, who achieved a true international reputation for the company, and set it in the position of dominance which it still occupies today. He was able to do this because he was a good businessman – and a very good friend.

He struck up the friendship in question with a young Corsican scholarship-holder at the military school of Brienne, east of Épernay, where Jean-Rémy travelled to sell wines. The student's name was Napoleon Bonaparte, and the friendship forged then lasted a lifetime. Its memorial can still be seen on the north side of Épernay's Avenue de Champagne, where two pretty houses frame a sunken formal garden leading to an orangery. This exquisite group of buildings was built as a staging post for Napoleon and his entourage on their way to and from the Austrian and Prussian fronts. The Emperor's own

'In victory you deserve (champagne);
in defeat you need it.'

NAPOLEON

Moët have adopted Dom Pérignon – though he died almost 30 years before the company's foundation – and named their cuvée de prestige after the wine-making monk.

tribute to this friendship came with his cross of the Légion d'Honneur, given personally to Jean-Rémy on Napoleon's last ever visit to Épernay – this time in full retreat from the advancing Russian forces.

Despite Jean-Rémy's close connections with Napoleon, he was able both to entertain the Emperor's enemies, such as Tsar Alexander I and Marshal Blücher of Prussia, and sell to those nations whose soldiers were dying at the hands of the French. After Napoleon's fall, Queen Victoria became a customer, as well as no fewer than 15 of her dukes. War was, in Moët's case, very definitely good for business.

The twentieth century has seen success for the company that is no less spectacular. Moët & Chandon (the company name changed after Pierre-Gabriel Chandon joined Victor Moët in 1832) is now the crown jewel of the giant LVMH group – or the spider at the centre of the web, depending on your point of view. Moët Hennessy-Louis Vuitton currently owns no less than seven of the largest champagne companies: Mercier, Ruinart, Veuve Clicquot, Canard-Duchêne, Henriot and Pommery, in addition to Moët. Its power within the region is enormous and on occasion ruthless, as shown by its unsentimental treatment of Lanson in 1990-91. LVMH bought Lanson then resold it – minus its vineyards.

Moët alone has 28km (over 17 miles) of cellars to house its stocks, and in those cellars you will find more bottles of champagne than there are French citizens in France: 86 million bottles, all told. It dominates exports, providing one out of every four bottles leaving France for consumption abroad. It is the largest-selling brand at home, too; and globally it sells more than twice as much as its nearest competitor, Mumm.

What of the wines? Perhaps inevitably, given the size of the company, they are inconsistent, with both the non-vintage Brut Impérial and the vintage Brut Impérial proving disappointing and satisfying on different occasions. At best, they are easy and straightforward champagnes, with sweet vanilla scents and well-balanced

Welcome relaxation for French soldiers in the trenches during World War One – thanks to a hamper of the local wine. The front line was fixed just north of Reims and hardly moved in four years.

flavours. A firm, plummy vintage rosé is also available.

Dom Pérignon, the most celebrated of all *cuvées de prestige*, is consistently good, with its flowery, apple-blossom aroma and vital, keen-edged fruit; tiny quantities of rosé Dom Pérignon are also produced.

ℳUMM

Bollinger, Deutz, Heidsieck, Krug, Mumm ... you could be looking through a German telephone directory rather than at a list of champagne producers. A startling number of Germans founded champagne firms, and many more came to work in Champagne.

Why? The answer lies in geography. A quick glance at the map of Europe shows that Champagne is France's nearest wine-producing region to the thirsty north of Germany, and Germany itself was the gateway to many of Champagne's key markets (Russia, Scandinavia) during the great expansion of the nineteenth century. It was more natural and useful for a lad from Cologne to go to work for a champagne company than it was for a lad from Marseille to do so.

Cologne, as it happens, was where the Mumms originated. Peter Arnold Mumm began trading as a wine merchant there in 1761. The city's position – on the Rhine, downstream of all the major German vineyards – made it ideal for supplying the drinkers of the north.

Sixty-six years later, in 1827, sparkling champagne was the marvel of the age, and the

Mumm's hugely successful Cordon Rouge is over 100 years old. These two posters, left and right, were introduced after World War One.

drinkers of the north wished to toast their successes in it like everyone else. Peter Arnold had died the year before, but his sons Jacobus, Gottlieb and Philipp, together with a Rhineland partner called Giesler, decided to open an office in Reims.

The company initially traded from the propitious address of 14 Rue de la Grosse Bouteille (Street of the Big Bottle), and bought its champagnes from outside suppliers: two in Avize, one in Aÿ, and one in Reims itself. But the first year of business was a great success – nearly 70,000 bottles were sold – so production began soon afterwards. A split later occurred, with one half of the company becoming Jules Mumm & Co, while the other half called itself GH Mumm & Co. GH prospered but Jules didn't, and by 1910 the two were back under one roof.

One reason behind GH Mumm's success was that it was one of the first companies to establish a brand of champagne, the famous Cordon Rouge. The idea had come from the father of Mumm's Paris agent, Welby Jourdan. 'Go ahead and decorate your bottle with the Légion d'Honneur. Sales will rocket!' wrote Jourdan's father to Georges Hermann von Mumm. The advice was heeded, in 1876; and the sales prediction proved correct. Cordon Rouge has the most instantly recognizable of all champagne labels, though few customers realize that its original inspiration was the red sash of France's greatest honour. The link has recently been renewed in the packaging of Grand Cordon, which has a real red ribbon round its neck – as did the first Cordon Rouge bottles. By the eve

CHAMPAGNE
G.H.MUMM&Cᵒ.

of World War One, primarily as a consequence of Cordon Rouge, Mumm was the largest champagne shipper, its three million bottles a year representing nine per cent of all champagne sales.

As soon as they had established themselves, most of Champagne's Germans became French citizens, but the Mumms were proud of their German origins and did not do this. The consequences for them were tragic.

By 1914, the Mumm family saw that war lay ahead in Europe and requested French citizenship, but the application had not been processed when World War One broke out. The director of the time, Hermann Mumm, behaved impeccably, staying in Reims to run the company and offering to pay his workers' wives their husbands' full salaries throughout the War, while the workers were fighting for France. But he was interned, and the company confiscated by the government.

At the end of the war, amid a general atmosphere of retribution, Mumm was sold to a consortium of French industrialists. The family understandably felt bitter about this, and carried on producing sparkling wines under their own name in Germany. They were prosecuted by Champagne Mumm. Revenge of a sort came with World War Two, when under the German occupation of Reims Godefroy Hermann Mumm retook control of the company, but this state of affairs was short-lived. The last of the Mumms left in 1945, and today the family produces still wines in the Rheingau.

Mumm's biggest-selling champagne suffers from the same problems that bedevils its chief rival, Moët's Brut Impérial: inconsistency. But when it is good, Cordon Rouge is a cheerful, well-rounded yet lively champagne. Cordon Rouge Vintage is generally drier, deeper and more impressive. The pink Cordon Rose, vintage-dated, is made in a nutty, firm style.

Mumm de Cramant is a non-vintage, *crémant* Blanc de Blancs made entirely from Chardonnay grapes grown in the *grand cru* village of Cramant, on the Côte des Blancs. Its bubbles are creamy on the tongue, and the

Mumm's Reims headquarters. Family control was severed by the war, rather than by the more usual business manoeuvres.

flavour is light, crisp and biscuity. The vintage Grand Cordon is very dry and thrusting, while the biggest of Mumm's champagnes is the vintage Cuvée René Lalou, named after a former chairman.

PERRIER-JOUËT

THINK OF PERRIER-JOUËT and you probably think of flowers: white anemones, say, on a celery-green stem, curling in an elegant arc around a green bottle. You are thinking of Belle Époque (Fleur de Champagne in the USA), Perrier-Jouët's famous *cuvée de prestige*.

It was first launched in 1969 at a party in a Paris night-club to mark Duke Ellington's seventieth birthday – though the actual bottle on which the design was based was almost as old as the great jazzman. The enamelled original had been created in 1902 by Émile Gallé, Art Nouveau glass-maker, but had lain forgotten in a cupboard for many years – until found by the company's cellarmaster in the 1960s. One of the directors saw the bottle's potential and set about adapting the design for commercial use.

The original has since been destroyed; it was on display in Fauchon, a luxury food and wine shop in Paris, when a terrorist bomb blast wrecked the premises.

Belle Époque has been such a success that Perrier-Jouët has created a Maison Belle Époque – part museum, part hospitality suite – at former owner Michel Budin's old home in Épernay. This lilac-pink house is an Art Nouveau shrine, full of intoxicatingly swirling lines, extravagant flower motifs, dreamy nymph-dragonflies, and lampshades that look as if they were fired in crème caramel.

What of the wine itself? One of the most surprising things is that it seems to shimmer with elegant, flowery Chardonnay, despite containing at least 50 per cent Pinot Noir. In this it is typical of the Perrier-Jouët style as a whole, which is very much that of an Épernay house.

The champagnes of Reims have traditionally been firm, sturdy and demanding, thanks to the great Pinots grown on the Montagne de Reims; those of Épernay have been lighter, finer and more fragrant, bearing the stamp of the Chardonnays from the Côte des Blancs, south of Épernay. In modern times these distinctions have been muddled, since any producer can now buy grapes from anywhere in the region with equal ease; Perrier-Jouët, indeed, might be said to be the last of the large Épernay houses to maintain a true 'Épernay' profile.

This profile can be seen right across the range, from Belle Époque down through the concentrated, complex, non-vintage Blason de France to the penetrating, lemony Grand Brut (vintage and non-vintage). Belle Époque and Blason de France

The Maison Belle Époque can be seen to the left of Perrier-Jouët's offices, on the far side of the Avenue de Champagne in Épernay.

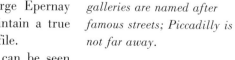

Perrier-Jouët's cellar galleries are named after famous streets; Piccadilly is not far away.

Perrier-Jouët is best known for its cuvée de prestige *Belle Époque. Its distinctive Art Nouveau bottle features in this festive painting, celebrating the Eiffel Tower's centenary.*

vintage in its natural state, without the sweetening of the usual heavy *dosage*. It appealed to him, and he thought he saw potential for a drier wine in the British market. Mr Burnes miscalculated, however, and the wine was a flop; but it did mark the beginning of a trend over the next two decades towards drier champagne. The Prince of Wales enjoyed the 1865 vintages of Bollinger and Ayala in 'Brut' form, and the 1874 vintage was supplied as a Brut to Britain by almost every shipper.

Nor did this failure damage the Perrier-Jouët name in Britain; three out of every four bottles the company produced crossed the Channel during most of the nineteenth century. It was even said to be the champagne drunk at the British court to celebrate Wellington's victory at Waterloo in 1815. If so, it must have been one of the very first bottles, since the company was only founded in 1811.

In recent times, America has taken over the running from Britain as the company's biggest market. Perhaps this is due to ownership by the North American-based Seagram multinational. A more likely explanation, though, is the glamour of the Belle Époque bottle, which has won it numerous screen appearances, and many more real-life appearances on glitzy restaurant tables.

both come in rosé versions, and here strawberry and apricot scents and flavours dominate. The slender finesse of Perrier-Jouët's champagnes put them at the other end of the style spectrum, say, to those of Krug or Veuve Clicquot.

Perrier-Jouët has had one major failure in its history about which it now speaks with pride. This occurred mid-way through the nineteenth century – at a time when champagne was still drunk in much, much sweeter form than it is today. In 1848 one Mr Burnes, a London wine merchant, had a chance to try a sample of the 1846

POL ROGER

POL ROGER WAS WINSTON CHURCHILL'S favourite champagne and champagne was his favourite drink. According to his bodyguard, Detective Inspector Thompson, he drank a pint of it daily – 'his only health fetish'. But he made Pol Roger his first choice following a meeting with Madame Odette Pol-Roger at a lunch given by Lady Diana Cooper at the British Embassy in Paris in November 1944. The city had been liberated over two months earlier and victory for the Allies now seemed certain. Odette was, by all accounts, a beautiful and fascinating woman, and on that occasion she was even more vivacious than usual. 'Elle etait pétillante,' said her nephew Christian de Billy. She sparkled.

The 70-year-old Churchill was captivated. From that moment Pol Roger champagne accompanied him on all his travels, specially bottled in imperial pints. He named his racehorse Odette Pol-Roger and, in due course, Pol Roger repaid the compliment by naming its *cuvée de prestige* after him; the Cuvée Sir Winston Churchill was launched with the 1975 vintage in the early 1980s. When Churchill died in 1965, the company, at Odette's request, printed a black border around the label of its non-vintage, a practice which continued for 25 years. It was then lightened to navy blue reflecting his former position as First Lord of the Admiralty.

This Épernay-based house has been family owned since its foundation in 1849 by Paul Roger ('Pol' was local dialect for Paul). By the time he died in 1899 the firm was so successful and his name so well known that his sons Maurice and Georges changed their surname to 'Pol-Roger' – not an easy task because such changes had to be specially authorized by the President.

No sooner had the company achieved this minor triumph than it suffered a major disaster: in early 1901 part of Pol Roger's cellars, which were being extended, collapsed. Two galleries and an above-ground warehouse went down, and with them 500 casks of wine and nearly one and a half million bottles of champagne. The company worked doggedly to make good the loss, and succeeded: between 1918 and 1934, for example, it sold more champagne in Britain than any other house.

In 1914 Maurice Pol-Roger was to need the fortitude that so sustained the company after this setback when, as mayor of Épernay, he helped the town survive seven days of German occupation. Falsely accused of severing

Pol Roger's offices in Épernay. Like most of today's leading champagne houses, Pol Roger was founded in the nineteenth century; it is one of the few that is still family owned.

gas and electricity supplies, he narrowly escaped execution and became a local hero. When he finally retired from the post in 1935, Épernay made him honorary mayor for life. After he died his son Jacques (Odette's husband) and nephew Guy took over, and the firm is now in the hands of Christian de Billy and Christian Pol-Roger, both great-grandsons of the founder.

The Pol Roger that Churchill enjoyed was a deeply flavoured, Pinot-rich, well-aged champagne: at his death in 1965 he was drinking the 1947, specially disgorged for him; and up until 1950 Pol Roger vintages contained between 70 and 80 per cent Pinot Noir. Since then the house style has lightened – partly because champagne is now drunk more as an aperitif than with meals. Yet the Pinot Noir proportion in the blend is still held at about 60 per cent, giving Pol Roger champagnes a full, firm flavour, with lots of round fruit.

There are five champagnes in the Pol Roger range – each distinguished by its neck foil. White foil speckled with gold belongs to the Brut non-vintage (Extra Dry in the UK): a champagne with a toasty cinnamon scent, lots of plummy fruit and a crisp finish. It is also available as Sec and Demi-Sec; the Demi-Sec is fresh and mouthfilling, its sweetness matched by appley acidity.

Bronze foil indicates Pol Roger's vintage champagne –

always a little more complex than the non-vintage, with a drier, more deeply fruity flavour. Lilac foil signifies the Rosé, and gold the Blanc de Blancs, both vintage dated. The Rosé has an earthy Pinot Noir scent, with cherry flavours and a lightly nutty finish. The Blanc de Blancs is more flowery and fragrant, but still comparatively round and full to taste.

Black foil signals the Cuvée Sir Winston Churchill, with its complex, earthy scents and solid yet graceful flavour. The *cuvée de prestige* for non-English-speaking markets is a creamier, more supple wine called Réserve Spéciale PR.

Odette Pol-Roger accompanying Churchill and the Duke of Norfolk (left) to the Brighton Races in 1951. Churchill named his racehorse after Odette – a telegram brings her news of another win.

POMMERY

IN 1858 VEUVE CLICQUOT was at the height of her glory. She had made a fortune, and was living in grand style in the turreted Château de Boursault. It was the year Reims received a state visit from Napoleon III, and the organization of this visit had been her responsibility. The queen of Champagne received the Emperor of France.

It was also the year in which Louis Pommery, director of the small firm of Pommery & Greno, died, leaving two children, Louis and Louise – and a widow. Madame Pommery had seen what Veuve Clicquot had been able to achieve; perhaps this lay behind her resolve to take over the running of her late husband's company. It was a small and insignificant one, specializing in selling still red wines to the north of France. When the Veuve Pommery died, 32 years later, her company was as important as Clicquot's, with huge export sales, fabulous cellars, and the most extravagant office buildings in Reims. Her daughter Louise, like Veuve Clicquot's daughter, had married into one of France's oldest aristocratic families, the Polignacs, and the company's superb, 300-hectare (741-acre) collection of vineyards was underway.

If you are staying in Reims, and have time to visit only one champagne house, choose Pommery. As you walk through the massive wrought-iron gates, you will be confronted by four extraordinary buildings. They don't seem to belong together, and they don't even seem to belong in France. This was Madame Pommery's tribute to her many British customers: a complex of buildings in 'Scottish baronial' style. Two of them, indeed, are partial copies of British originals: Inveraray Castle in Argyll and Mellerstain in Berwickshire.

Underneath these buildings lie some of the most spectacular cellars in Champagne, and they also were the product of Madame Pommery's remarkably inventive mind. Previously the firm's cellars had been near Reims cathedral in the centre of town; as the company expanded rapidly under her directorship, they became too small. Beyond Reims' border was a hilly area called the Butte St-Niçaise. It was here that the Romans had excavated the chalk they used as building stone, and the caves they created still existed.

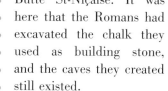

Part of Pommery's complex in Reims, distinguished by its 'Scottish' architecture. The building on the immediate left houses an ultra-modern fermentation hall.

Madame Pommery, like other Champagne widows, took over her husband's firm.

Madame Pommery connected and refurbished 120 of the chalk pits, stretching 19km (11 miles) in length, providing the company simultaneously with enormous storage space and a major tourist attraction. Each one of these huge vaulted chambers – where the pick-marks of the Roman workers are still visible in the chalk as it funnels up to a tiny skylight at the top – makes an impressive sight; together, they form a magnificent white labyrinth. Madame Pommery's natural sense of drama added a grand 116-step staircase leading down to the cellars, and she commissioned ambitious *bas-reliefs* – pictures cut into the chalk walls – from the artist Henri Navlet.

After Madame Pommery died, her son Louis took over the running of the company, and after Louis's death in 1907 the company passed to the Polignac family. Today it is owned by the LVMH group, but Prince Alain de Polignac continues to make the wines.

The Pommery style of champagne is lively, elegant and pretty – champagne in a summer frock. What it lacks in depth and texture, it makes up for in grace and charm.

Brut Royal is the name of Pommery's biggest-selling non-vintage: it is a very pale yellow-gold in colour, with light, zesty aromas and a fresh flavour. Although Brut Royal is as round and lively as a Cox's apple, it has no green or malic edges. Pommery's Brut Rosé is made by maceration, using plenty of Pinot Noir and Meunier for fruit and depth, with up to one-third Chardonnay for finesse. It has backbone to accompany food, but also the sprightliness of a good aperitif rosé.

The Vintage Brut has a formal symmetry to it: half Pinot Noir, half Chardonnay, all of it from Pommery's 100 per cent-rated vineyards. It has a fuller, firmer flavour than the Brut Royal, yet no less charm. The range is crowned by the vintage-dated Louise Pommery, named after Madame Pommery rather than her daughter; it has an appealing apple-blossom fragrance

The plan of Pommery's cellar network, 30 metres underground. The long galleries, named after the world's cities, are of nineteenth-century origin; the original Roman-excavated chalk pits are the small cellars to the right.

and tingling delicacy of flavour; also available as a rosé.

Large bottles, up to salmanazar size, are a Pommery speciality; unusually, all the second fermentations are carried out in the bottles themselves, which are then disgorged, dosed, corked and labelled by hand. Pommery is also the only one of the *grandes marques* to continue to distil its own Marc de Champagne.

LOUIS ROEDERER

ALTHOUGH BRITAIN WAS THE MOST important export market for champagne throughout much of the nineteenth century, next in importance was Russia. Two companies dominated sales there: Veuve Clicquot and Roederer. Their success was built on the verve of star salesmen – Louis Bohne for Clicquot, and for Roederer Monsieur Krafft. Krafft joined the company in 1836, and within a few years had placed Louis Roederer champagne on the table of that most conspicuous of consumers, the Tsar.

Tsar Nicholas I was pleased with his champagne, and remained a loyal customer. By our standards, the wine was unbelievably sweet, with about five or six times as much sugar as the sweetest of today's champagnes, and sometimes with a dollop of brandy or Chartreuse added for good measure, too.

Alexander II replaced his father on the Russian throne in 1855, and saw no reason to change his champagne supplier. Indeed, he took more interest in the subject than his father did, and had a special *cuvée* prepared each year by his cellarmaster, who would visit Reims to oversee the blending.

Yet the Tsar still felt something required improvement. He looked down his table at the bottles swaddled in napkins (a practice that is still common in Eastern Europe) and

Tsar Alexander II, who commissioned Cristal.

realized his champagne looked no different from anybody else's. What he needed was a special bottle.

This was how the famous Cristal came into being, in 1876-77. Roederer borrowed the idea of a clear-glass bottle from Eugène Mercier, who had produced one for Napoleon III. The Roederer version, however, was in crystal glass – glass so strong that it needed no punt (the strengthening indentation at the bottom). The success of Cristal increased Russian sales for Roederer, which was a mixed blessing for, when the Revolution came in 1917, the company lost 80 per cent of its market overnight: a massive setback.

It took a long time for Roederer to recover from this blow, and the woman who helped the company do so was Camille Olry-Roederer, one of the great champagne

Roederer's substantial vineyard holdings, supplying 75 per cent of its grape needs, are the envy of its rivals.

widows of the twentieth century. She was the wife of the great-nephew of the original Louis Roederer and she directed the company single-handedly over 42 years.

During this time, one of the cleverest moves she made was to build up Roederer's 180-hectare (445-acre) estate. It now provides three-quarters of Roederer's needs, and is one reason why the company has been able to remain independent – and highly profitable. Fifty-five hectares (136 acres) of these vineyards are on the Montagne de Reims; 50 hectares (123 acres) are in the Vallée de la Marne; and the rest are on the Côte des Blancs; their combined rating on the *échelle des crus* is 98 per cent. This is a perfect recipe for champagne. The purchases were all the more canny since they came at a time when most companies were selling off their vineyards – something they now bitterly regret.

Camille Olry-Roederer was well known for her stylish interpretation of the role of businesswoman. She dressed finely, and glittered with gold and diamond jewellery – yet always wore a man's wristwatch, 'to give masculine authority', as she put it. When she travelled on business, she took a thick dossier containing every document she might need, yet never forgot her needlework. Her daughter Claude is company president today, and grandson Jean-Claude Rouzaud is managing director.

Roederer's champagnes may not be as sweet as they were in the nineteenth century, yet they are still among the richest on the market, and are a recommended choice if you find many other champagnes sharp and over-acid. The Brut Premier, a non-vintage, accounts for seven out of every ten bottles of Roederer champagne, and is the best example of the full, firm house style. This is not just a question of grams of sugar, but is also due to Roederer's policy of keeping very large stocks of reserve wines – a higher proportion, in relation to sales, than any other house.

The Brut Rosé and Brut Vintage are built in the same comfortable style as Brut Premier, while the vintage-dated Blanc de Blancs is lighter and very creamy, almost

Roederer's offices in Reims. Behind the impressive façade are fermenting tanks and wood-aged reserve wines.

a *crémant*. Cristal varies according to the vintage, but is usually an elegant and penetrating champagne of high quality – though seldom worth the price differential with Brut Premier. A Cristal Rosé is also produced.

Veuve Clicquot-Ponsardin

THE MOST FAMOUS PORTRAIT of the Widow Clicquot, by Léon Cogniet, shows her in a large, red-backed arm-chair, somewhere in the warm gloom of the Château de Boursault – her home for the last 20 years of her life. In the painting, her square, thick-set features frame a stout and unblinking gaze. Her finger is positioned at the top of one of the pages of her open book, as if the artist had asked her to look up suddenly and she was unwilling to lose her place. The carefully arranged ringlets, and the chiffon at her throat and wrists, are there because fashion required them, but there is no trace of vanity in her eyes. In its place is a calm certainty about the world.

Nicole-Barbe Clicquot (née Ponsardin) was widowed in 1805 at the age of 27, when her daughter Clémentine was just eight years old. Her father was a leading textile merchant in Reims. In 1798 she had married François Clicquot, whose own father traded in both wool and wine. Their wedding ceremony took place in a champagne cellar, not as an extravagant and romantic gesture but simply because at that time, soon after the French Revolution, churches had not yet opened again for public worship.

After her husband's early death, her father-in-law Philippe immediately made plans to sell the business that he had founded in 1772, and which his son had so recently taken over. Yet shortly afterwards he died too, his heart attack no doubt precipitated by the shock of his son's untimely death. What did life hold for the young widow? She and her daughter would never be poor; after a reasonable interval, she might marry again, and perhaps have more children. That would be what society expected of her.

Instead she did the unexpected. The funerals completed, the tears dried, she reopened the business, taking as her collaborators the brilliant German salesman Louis

Left The first lady of fizz – and the first great champagne widow – Veuve Clicquot, in the famous portrait by Léon Cogniet. As well as wine, her business interests included textiles and banking.

Right Only 60 of Reims' 14,150 houses remained habitable at the end of World War One; Clicquot's Hôtel de Marc was one of them. Ninety per cent of the town was destroyed.

Bohne and the blender Jérôme Fourneaux. Between the establishment of Veuve Clicquot-Ponsardin, Fourneaux & Cie at the end of 1806 and her death in 1866, she created a great and enormously profitable champagne house. She invented the system of *remuage*, one of the key processes in the making of champagne, and she even found time to establish a bank, to buy and sell wool, and run a spinning mill.

After her death the business, and a portion of the vineyards, were left to her chief partner Édouard Werlé, which is why this name appears beneath the Clicquot-crowned star on the company's labels and corks. Veuve Clicquot's daughter Clémentine was a shy and timid girl who had married a charming but dissolute aristocrat Comte Louis de Chevigné. The Widow knew that leaving the business in the hands of Clémentine and Louis would have been a disaster.

Werlé, by contrast, was a businessman of genius, who steadily built up sales throughout Europe, sensing that too exclusive a reliance on the Russian market was unwise. Werlé crowned the Widow's work.

The house remained in the hands of descendants of the Werlé family until, after a succession of business manoeuvres, it became part of the LVMH (Moët Hennessy-Louis Vuitton) group in 1987.

Clicquot has its roots at Bouzy. It was there that Philippe Clicquot first began trading as what would now be called a *récoltant-manipulant* (grower-producer), and today in the same village the company still owns about ten per cent of its estate. Some of the best Pinot Noir in Champagne grows at Bouzy and the Clicquot house style is built on a firm base of Pinot Noir.

The Brut non-vintage, with its distinctive, light orange label and its finely scrolled lettering, is composed of 56 per cent Pinot Noir, with the balance made up of 16 per cent Pinot Meunier and the rest Chardonnay. There is plenty of sweet-edged fruit on the aroma, while the flavour is deep and round, with musky pear flavours. A Demi-Sec is also available.

Clicquot's vintage-dated Rosé, too, is rich in Pinot (up to 70 per cent). The 1983 version has a handsome coppery colour, with complex, leafy scents and a deep, dry,

cutting flavour. The 1983 white Vintage Reserve is a less Pinot-influenced wine, though Pinot still accounts for the majority of the blend; it is full and serious but lacks grace and charm. The vintage wines are given between five and six years on their second fermentation lees.

At the top of the pyramid sits – who else? – La Grande Dame, Clicquot's *cuvée de prestige*. The 1985 has a deep, dry, arrestingly fruity flavour, very sturdy and strong. It will age well, if stored correctly, and is an ideal champagne for food.

A VCP view of the road to Reims – and to Clicquot champagne; on the skyline, Reims cathedral.

OTHER HOUSES AND GROWERS

CHAMPAGNE MAY BE HOME TO FRANCE'S largest wine-producing conglomerate (the houses grouped together under the LVMH banner), but it also acts as a stage for the endeavours of a huge number of smaller enterprises. These vary from family-run houses of considerable size and distinction, like Taittinger or Laurent-Perrier, to growers with a few hectares of vines who make their own champagne rather than sell grapes to large companies.

AYALA, based in Aÿ, traces it unusual name back to Raphael de Ayala, the son of a Colombian diplomat. He acquired vineyards as part of his wife's dowry, and Ayala was created in 1860 to sell the champagne they produced. Today the company is owned by the Ducellier family. It favours Pinot Noir in its blends, and produces concentrated, serious champagnes at a very fair price.

BARANCOURT, formed in 1969 by three growers, is based in the great Pinot Noir-producing village of Bouzy; its best vintage wines (such as the magnificent, sombre Cuvée des Fondateurs 1985) are splendid illustrations of how champagne can suggest dark plums or even chocolate when it contains a high proportion of black grapes.

BESSERAT DE BELLEFON has, since the 1920s, specialized in producing *crémant* champagnes, and its Cuvée des Moines continues to be made in this style, though the term *crémant* is no longer used. The company was dis-

membered in 1990, following a number of changes of ownership. Marne et Champagne now owns the name, while Rémy-Cointreau holds the stocks and cellars.

BILLECART-SALMON is a small house based in Mareuil-sur-Aÿ. It is still owned by the Billecart-Salmon family, who have lived in Mareuil since the sixteenth century. The house speciality is the use of a cool, slow first fermentation. This gives a very light, lacy style, particularly impressive in the Brut Rosé and Blanc de Blancs wines.

CANARD-DUCHÊNE'S wines are inconsistent in quality, but the company occasionally produces good blends at an inexpensive price. It is a member of the LVMH group.

DE CASTELLANE is a company best known for its extraordinary tower: this dominates the Épernay skyline from its position mid-way up the Avenue de Champagne. The champagnes of De Castellane attract less attention, though the prestige *cuvée* Vintage Commodore is very pure, subtle and rewarding. The Nonancourt family of Laurent-Perrier controls De Castellane.

DEUTZ is a small, much-admired house based in Aÿ. This admiration has been won for its complicated and unusual champagnes, always well aged, and for the superb results it has achieved with its sparkling wine co-enterprises in California and New Zealand.

GOSSET, another of Aÿ's small, traditional champagne-producers, is in fact the oldest company in the region. It traces its roots back to 1584, when Pierre Gosset began to sell his wines under his own name. Antoine Gosset, the fourteenth generation of the family, still runs the company, which produces fine, handmade champagnes full of lush, toasty-rich fruit. Rosés are a speciality.

ALFRED GRATIEN is a quiet, unshowy champagne house, run by the Seydoux family. Highly traditional methods, such as first fermentation in wood for all wines and long lees ageing, give complex, full, serious champagnes, much enjoyed in Britain. Gratien systematically avoids malolactic fermentation for its wines.

HEIDSIECK-MONOPOLE, one of the three houses descended from the original Heidsieck, founded by Florens-Louis in 1785, has traditionally produced firm, full champagnes, marked by Pinot Noir. These have lightened and freshened a little since the company came under Mumm's ownership in 1972, but remain striking, characterful, richly flavoured – and undervalued. The company owns a famous Champagne landmark, the Moulin de Verzenay. This, the region's only windmill, was used as an observation post during World War One.

HENRIOT is a modestly sized, high quality company, providing classy champagnes of sensuous, creamy complexity. The company was founded in 1808 by a minor champagne widow, Veuve Appoline Henriot, whose grandson worked for many years with 'Champagne Charlie', Charles-Camille Heidsieck. This association inspired his present-day descendant, Joseph Henriot, to write a novel about Charles-Camille called *Champagne Charlie*; the novel has since been filmed. Henriot is now part of the LVMH group, for whom Joseph Henriot works in a senior role.

JACQUESSON is a small, family-owned company based in the little village of Dizy. This was the house for whom the first Krug, Joseph, once worked, and in its heyday (in the early nineteenth century) it was one of the biggest and grandest of all, producing three times as much champagne as it does today. It now concentrates on making modest quantities of elegant, delicate champagne, full of finesse and charm. Its Blanc de Blancs is a benchmark Chardonnay.

LAURENT-PERRIER is a family-owned company which has proved that the support of multinational backers is not essential for sustained growth. Until World War Two, this was a very small house indeed; since then, under the guidance of Bernard de Nonancourt, it has expanded dramatically, and won an enviable reputation for its delicate, fresh range. If you wish to meet the challenge of a completely unsweetened champagne, Laurent-Perrier's Ultra Brut is more regularly successful than most of its rivals; and the ordinary non-vintage Brut is long and elegant, reliably good. The *cuvée de prestige*, Grand Siècle, is sold vintage-dated in the USA, while in Europe it is blended from three or more different vintages, giving greater complexity.

MARNE ET CHAMPAGNE is the second largest champagne-producer of all, despite having been founded as recently as 1933. The reason why its name is so little known is that it never appears on bottles: the company specializes in supplying 'own label' or 'private label' champagnes, and also supplies other champagne houses with stocks. Marne et Champagne has a number of brands of its own, the most widely distributed of which are labelled with the name of A Rothschild. It has also recently acquired the Besserat de Bellefon brand, and the Lanson brands, stocks and cellars. The company is controlled by its 90-year-old founder, Gaston Burtin.

BRUNO PAILLARD, sometime export consultant to Marne et Champagne and part-time broker, founded his own champagne house in 1981. The Paillard style is light, spare and elegant.

JOSEPH PERRIER is the last champagne house to remain in Châlons-sur-Marne, once home to thirteen or more different companies (including Jacquesson). The Cuvée Royal Brut, with its distinctive lemon-yellow label, continues to please those who like a generous Pinot-rich champagne, full of ripe fruit.

PHILIPPONNAT, still run by the Collard-Philipponnat family (though now owned by liqueur-producer Marie Brizard), produces full, complex and subtle champagnes, often with a hint of pineapple to them. The company owns one of Champagne's most famous vineyards, the Clos des Goisses, sited on a flat-topped hillside next to the Marne-au-Rhin canal. The wine produced from this vineyard is soft yet intense, and ages superbly. Philipponnat's creamy, perfumed rosé is no less delicious.

PIPER-HEIDSIECK, now part of the Rémy-Cointreau group, produces zesty-lemony champagnes requiring time to show at their best. This is a house that, like Lanson and Gratien, avoids malolactic fermentation, leaving some of the wines in the range rather hard when first released – but they achieve depth with age.

RUINART was founded by linen-trader Nicolas Ruinart in 1729. He gave his customers bottles of champagne as business gifts from time to time; they evidently liked them, and gradually champagne took over in importance from linen. During the 1950s, Ruinart worked in association with Château Mouton-Rothschild, and in 1963 it was taken over by Moët & Chandon, making it part of the LVMH group today. It has some of the most spectacular of all Champagne's cellars, in the *crayères* area of Reims. Ruinart's blends are vibrant, crisp and sinewy, and Chardonnay is prominent in all of them, even the Rosé. The Blanc de Blancs is very fine.

SALON, a small company based in Le Mesnil-sur-Oger and controlled by Laurent Perrier, produces only one wine: a very dry, vintage Blanc de Blancs of great severity and distinction. All of the grapes come from the *grand cru* Le Mesnil, and the wine is only produced in the best years. Sales are limited to a mere 60,000 bottles per year, and the wine requires long ageing.

TAITTINGER is the direct descendant of one of the oldest of all champagne houses, Fourneaux, founded in 1734; the company was acquired by the Taittinger family in 1931. Pierre Taittinger, who made the purchase, came from Alsace, but remained in Champagne after he had served as a soldier there during World War One.

The company has extensive vineyards, with over 250 hectares (618 acres), including substantial holdings in the Aube. It also has good Côte des Blancs vineyards; there is an overall preponderance of Chardonnay.

Taittinger champagnes are made to a high standard, and are marked, as the vineyard disposition would suggest, by Chardonnay characteristics: flowery scent, elegance and penetrating length. The Blanc de Blancs *cuvée de prestige*, Comtes de Champagne, memorably exemplifies these characteristics; the Brut Réserve, however, can be a little thin. Taittinger's Vintage Collection, a non-Blanc de Blancs *cuvée de prestige*, comes in champagne's most eye-catching bottles.

DE VENOGE, damned with faint praise by the nineteenth-century writer Vizetelly as 'a great ... manufacturer of common-class champagne', has worked hard in recent years to re-upholster its image. In taste terms, this means that the traditional De Venoge softness and creaminess has been lightened and refined. The house style, nevertheless, remains one based on Pinot Noir of rich and toasty character, and this is best seen in the Brut Vintage and the Rosé Crémant. De Venoge is one of the few houses to produce a Blanc de Noirs – in this case as an elegant non-vintage Brut.

CO-OPERATIVES AND GROWERS

Among co-operative-produced champagnes, names to watch out for include **Saint-Gall,** from the large Avize-based co-operative Union Champagne; **Jacquart,** a co-operative whose status has recently been altered to that of a private company; the small **Mailly-Champagne**; **Le Mesnil**, sited on the Côte des Blancs where some of its members own 100 per cent-rated vineyards; **Palmer,** based in Reims; **Nicolas Feuillatte**, produced by the Centre Vincole de la Champagne at Chouilly; **Paul Goerg**, from the small Côte des Blancs co-operative La Goutte d'Or at Vertus, and **Pierre Vaudon**, based in Avize. The best blends from each of these are well worth trying. Individual growers' champagnes are not yet widely exported, but look out for **Château de Boursault, Hostomme, Jacques Selosse** and **Vilmart**.

SYNDICAT DE GRANDES MARQUES DE CHAMPAGNE

The largest champagne houses belong to this grouping established in 1964. It consists of the following houses:

Ayala	Massé
Billecart-Salmon	Mercier
Bollinger	Moët & Chandon
Canard-Duchêne	Montebello
Charles & Prieur	Mumm
Charles Heidsieck/Henriot	Perrier-Jouët
Deutz & Geldermann	Piper-Heidsieck
Heidsieck-Monopole	Pol Roger
Joseph Perrier	Pommery & Greno
Krug	Ruinart
Lanson	Salon
Laurent-Perrier	Taittinger/Irroy
Louis Roederer	Veuve Clicquot-Ponsardin

ENJOYING CHAMPAGNE

There is something faintly absurd about describing how to enjoy champagne. It is rather like telling people how to laugh, or how to have fun on a luxury holiday. Champagne is always a treat whenever it is served, and it is normally served at times of relaxation and celebration. Enjoyment should be effortless.

Yet champagne can undoubtedly be served well, or served badly. As it is one of the world's most expensive wines, to serve champagne badly is unwise, for you may be wasting money as well as spoiling the party. If you serve it well, however, it will seem to you the best of wines, worth every penny, and your celebration will be all the warmer for it.

A detail of an 1894 poster by Cheret advertising the Taverne Olympia – a famous Paris night club. It captures all of champagne's gaiety and joie de vivre.

BUYING AND STORING

GOOD CHAMPAGNE TASTES WONDERFUL in Champagne. Served at twilight in winter, when the vineyards and beet fields dissolve in cold, rosy mist, as the drinker stands in a spacious drawing room over the deep chalk caves in which the wine matured and from which it was brought a few hours earlier: these are the ideal conditions for champagne to show at its best. It will taste clean, fresh, foamy, scented, incisive, rousing, inspiring – altogether more than the sum of its parts.

Handle with care

Good champagne does not always taste wonderful outside Champagne. Every honest champagne enthusiast will tell you that bottles of impeccable pedigree may prove disappointing after they have been opened. To some extent, this is due to 'bottle variation', common to all wines. Wine is a living thing, placed in a small con-

Krug's cellars provide a perfect environment for ageing champagne: darkness, stillness and a constant cool temperature are the key factors.

tainer; what happens after the container is sealed is never entirely predictable. But the main reason is that champagne is a fragile and sensitive wine, more susceptible than most to the shocks of transport and, especially, poor storage.

If, for example, a bottle of champagne was placed in a south-facing shop window during a sunny spring month, the combined effects of direct sunlight and huge daily temperature variations would spoil it irreversibly within a week or two. This is a dramatic example. Less dramatic but equally sure ways of damaging champagne include storing it upright in centrally heated rooms for a long time or exposing it to ordinary interior lighting, again for a lengthy period. Many champagnes are now packed in individual boxes which can prevent the wines acquiring the mousy or sweaty taint known in French as *goût de la lumière* (taste of light), but such boxes do not protect the wine from adverse temperature conditions. One of the keys to enjoying champagne, therefore, is to buy it either as young as possible, or from a supplier you know has stored it properly.

Keeping it dark

Once you have brought home your champagne, you have two options: drink it or store it.

If you are going to drink it within a week or two, you need not worry unduly about storage. Simply avoid the obviously unsuitable places: next to stoves, cookers or radiators, anywhere where it could get knocked over, or anywhere where the sun will sweep across it. Even a month or two should not make much difference, provided the wine is left in a dark and peaceful spot without large temperature variations.

If, however, you wish to store the wine for longer than a couple of months, you should keep it in complete darkness, undisturbed, and at a steady temperature. A cellar is ideal; but if you don't have a cellar, put it in a cupboard that is seldom opened, or under a bed that is seldom used. Choose somewhere as central and as low in the house as possible, so that daily temperature fluctuations are minimized. Make sure that the wine is lying flat.

For long-term storage – for a year or more – a proper cellar is essential. Champagne must have permanent darkness, stillness, and a constant, cool temperature if it is to age successfully. Most good wine merchants can arrange correct cellar storage for you if you have no cellar of your own.

To age or not to age

In principle, champagne houses only release their wines when they are ready to drink. The *appellation* regulations stipulate certain minimum ageing periods, and most of the exporting houses will exceed these by a comfortable margin. So no champagne actually needs to be stored further.

However, many champagne enthusiasts maintain that even non-vintage champagne gains in composure and harmony by a six- to eight-month storage period, and that all vintage champagnes should be aged for between one and three years following their release for similar motives. The wines may be technically ready when they leave France, but their full potential requires extra age. Indeed a number of importers ensure that all the champagnes are given six months' 'landing age' after arrival. Why? 'It rounds it up, settles it down, softens it out and makes it a more complete wine,' says Michael Druitt, the London agent for Perrier-Jouët. You can achieve much the same effect for yourself by carrying out further ageing on the champagnes you buy.

Old champagne, however, is an acquired taste. 'Old' might be defined as ten years from the vintage date in the case of vintage champagne, or five years from the purchase date in the case of non-vintage champagne. If

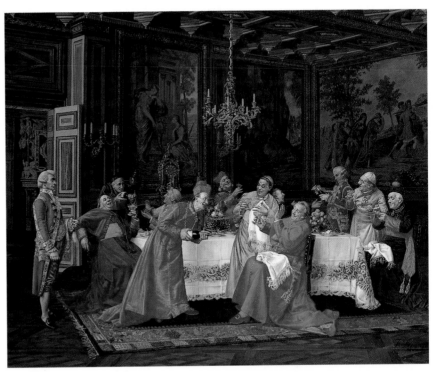

The Battle of the Champagne Corks *by nineteenth-century artist François Brunery is a perfect example of how* not *to handle champagne.*

you are thinking about ageing champagne for this length of time or more, you should make sure that you have 'acquired the taste'.

And what is the taste? On the plus side, any harshness the wine had will have gone, and the aromas and flavours will be rich, enticing, gracious. On the minus side, the sparkle leaves the glass more rapidly after pouring, and much of the champagne will be drunk more or less as a still wine. If you like a crisp, zingy, aperitif style, you may feel that the champagne has lost edge and bite. For a lively celebration, old champagne may indeed disappoint; but at a quiet dinner, with time to listen to the wine and search out its charms, the virtues of age become pleasingly apparent.

SERVING CHAMPAGNE

THERE ARE TWO WELL-KNOWN STYLES of champagne glass – and they are very different from each other. The first is a broad, flat, short-stemmed glass, the kind of glass you could cradle in the palm of your hand. This is the *coupe*, which was first produced in the late 1600s, before champagne got its sparkle. The most famous version was modelled and moulded on the breast of Marie-Antoinette. Four originals were made, in Sèvres porcelain, to furnish the queen's Dairy Temple at Rambouillet; one only remains. Milk white, with a delicately rounded nipple at the base, it is supported on a tripod topped by three goats' heads. As a historical curiosity, it is admirable; as a model for a champagne glass, it is a disaster. The large surface of wine exposed to the air releases the bubbles rapidly and dissipates their aromas, while the temptation to cradle the glass in one's hand ensures that the wine heats up rapidly.

Champagne requires a *flute* – in other words, a tall, slender glass. Ideally, the bottom of the bowl should end in a point, and the top of the bowl should be narrower than its centre, giving it a shape that resembles an elongated, Art Nouveau tulip. A tall stem and narrow base adds to the overall elegance. In such a glass, the aromas will be concentrated, the mousse swirling and sustained, the chill tenacious, and the wine presented to the tongue in a narrow stream that intensifies its delicious impact. (*Coupes* are best kept for ice cream and fruit salad.)

The weaving ribbons of fine-beaded bubbles, and the snowy crown of foam at the wine's edge, are both part of champagne's delight, so try to use clear glass rather than cut or tinted glass in order to appreciate these attractions, and the wine's colour, fully.

The chill factor

The best way to chill champagne thoroughly is to give it between two and four hours in the refrigerator, the exact length of time depending on the initial temperature of the wine. If you are in a hurry, half an hour in the freezer will produce a rapid, though incomplete, chill. Half an hour in an ice-bucket, filled with a mixture of water and ice, is more efficient – and it will not have explosive results if you forget about the champagne (as might happen with the bottle in the freezer).

The chilling of champagne has two purposes. First, champagne

The shallow coupe *has always been a popular glass, but the slender* flute *captures champagne's sparkle and aromas much more successfully.*

tastes much better at 8°C than it does at 18°C. The second purpose of chilling is to subdue the sparkle: it is easier to open the bottle in a controlled and safe manner when the pressure has been reduced.

Opening time

Watch the post-presentation antics after any Formula One motor race for an example of how not to open champagne. Do not agitate the bottle violently; do not send the cork flying as far and as fast as it will go (at motor races, the corks are removed before the bottles are given to the drivers as a sensible safety precaution); do not spray everyone in sight with whooshing jets of champagne. Not, that is, if you actually want to drink and savour the wine.

As this magazine illustration shows, champagne is best served chilled and then kept cool in an ice bucket.

OPENING A BOTTLE OF CHAMPAGNE

1 *Always point the bottle away from your body, and never point it at anyone else. Unwrap the top of the foil and remove the wire muzzle carefully.*

2 *Put one hand over the cork and grip it tight. Hold the bottle near its base with the other hand and gently turn the bottle. Keep the bottle at an angle of 45°.*

3 *The turning motion frees the cork which you can now slowly ease out. Keep holding the cork while you do this and keep the bottle at an angle.*

4 *Pour a little champagne into each glass carefully, as the foam will be very frothy. Let the foam die down and then top up to the half-way mark.*

CHAMPAGNE AND FOOD

CHAMPAGNE DOES NOT HAVE TO BE DRUNK with food. Indeed most champagne is probably drunk on its own, before a meal. Yet if there are just two of you, or if the bottle of champagne is a big one, or if the first bottle is so good you can't resist a second ... you may wish to sit down and eat a meal accompanied by champagne.

The ideal partner

Champagne makes a good partner to certain foods. Fish is chief among these: all fish finds the delicacy and vivifying acidity that it needs in champagne. Cream or

butter sauces are balanced out by the freshness and liveliness of the wine, while the bubbles add to the sense of lightness, as if you had served the fish with a kind of liquid soufflé. Seafood, too, is delicious with champagne, though prepared seafood dishes (sauced scallops, say) are perhaps more rewarding as partners than raw seafood on the shell. Oysters and champagne, or indeed caviar and champagne, are more impressive as statements of wealth or *joie de vivre* than as combinations.

Light, white meats can be enjoyable with champagne, particularly chicken dishes from the classic French repertoire. As with fish, the best combinations are those where the dish itself is rich but not overly assertive. For example, chicken breast served with a herby cream sauce would be memorably partnered by champagne, for the wine would make a contribution (primarily of acidity) to the dish that could come from nowhere else. Jointed chicken served *à la provençale* – swimming in tomatoes and peppers and olives and garlic – would be less successful, however, as the acidity of the tomatoes and peppers, and the heady southern flavours, would mean that the champagne's own acidity would be superfluous, and its biscuity complexities disagreeable.

Light red meat, plainly prepared, can work well with rosé champagne. Lamb noisettes or cutlets, grilled or sautéed, are perfect with rosé champagne in which the earthy, fruity flavour of Pinot Noir and Pinot Meunier is dominant; the same is true of game dishes based on pheasant, partridge and rabbit. By contrast hare, venison and beef generally overwhelm champagne, and are better served with a rich red wine.

Finishing courses

Few cheeses accompany champagne well, and some – like ripe examples of the Champagne region's most famous cheese, Brie – make it taste extraordinarily

Le repas au champagne – *a meal with champagne throughout – shows the wine's versatility.*

unpleasant. Approach the cheese and champagne combination with extreme caution, and begin with rosé champagne in preference to white.

Dry champagnes taste emaciated and hard with desserts, but sweeter champagnes of around the demi-sec level are delicious, especially with fruit-based patisserie. The sweetness of the champagne seems to disappear when lined up against the dessert itself, and the sparkle, acidity and round fruit of demi-sec champagne can reawaken the most jaded appetite.

Finally, if you can afford it, champagne is a wonderful wine to cook with. A reduction of champagne with cream and fish stock, finished with butter, is one of the most memorable of all sauces for fine white fish, and a half glass of champagne added to any ordinary white wine reduction will bring distinction to a sauce.

Champagne cocktails

It is hard to reach any conclusion but that mixing champagne with other alcoholic or non-alcoholic drinks and flavourings is a waste. Grand Marnier, Angostura bitters, brandy, orange juice, Guinness ... these are strong flavours, much stronger than that of champagne itself, and all the subtleties and nuances that you have paid for will be squandered. Unless you are so wealthy that it simply does not matter whether or not you use champagne, choose a good-quality sparkling wine in preference to champagne for the following drinks.

Buck's Fizz is a simple mixture of orange juice and champagne, in approximately equal proportions. Other fruit juices may also be used; peach juice and champagne is known as a Bellini. Replace the fruit juice with Guinness and you have the bizarre Black Velvet.

The classic champagne cocktail is little more than a mild act of vandalism against the wine. Put a lump of sugar in a wine glass and soak it with Angostura bitters. Squeeze the aromatic oil out of two or three pieces of lemon peel into the glass (the best tool for this is a garlic press that has *never* been used for garlic), then add a

Champagne cocktails don't do justice to champagne, but they are seldom out of fashion.

lump of ice. Fill the glass with champagne, stir cautiously, and drop in an unsqueezed piece of lemon peel. Variations can be effected using orange peel and a teaspoon of Grand Marnier. Many versions of the classic champagne cocktail include a teaspoon of brandy.

A champagne cobbler requires a tumbler. Mix together a teaspoon of sugar syrup, a teaspoon of Curaçao and a glass of champagne. Fill the tumbler with ice, pour over the mixture and top with slices of summer fruit. For a champagne julep, put a lump of sugar and a few mint leaves into a tumbler, and gently press the mint against the sugar to extract its flavour. Add ice, and pour on the champagne. Finish with slices of fruit if you wish.

ℐNDEX

AUTHOR'S ACKNOWLEDGEMENTS

I would like to thank the Comité Interprofessionnel du Vin de Champagne and its Public Relations Director, Philippe le Tixerant, for enabling me to make two research visits to the region in the autumn of 1990; Penny Bool and Maarit Pope of the Champagne Bureau in London for much administrative and consultative help; also Colonel François Bonal of Épernay, John Collard, Véronique Foureur, and Dr Richard Scrivener of the British Geological Survey.

Editorial Director Sandy Carr
Art Director Douglas Wilson
Editor Catherine Dell
Art Editor Sally Powell
Wine Consultant Wink Lorch
DTP Alan Duff
Editorial Assistants Siobhan Bremner, Annie Galpin
Design Assistant Jason Vrakas
Indexer Naomi Good
Map Lorraine Harrison
Illustrations Coral Mula (pages 39, 91)
Colour Tinting Gillie Newman